JACK OF FABLES

THE END

A
NIMBLE PICTURES/VERTIGO
PRODUCTION

JACK OF FABLES

THE END

Bill Willingham
& Matthew Sturges
WRITERS

Tony Akins
Russ Braun
PENCILLERS

Andrew Pepoy Dan Green
Tony Akins Bill Reinhold
INKERS

Daniel Vozzo
COLORIST

Todd Klein
LETTERER

Brian Bolland
COVER ART &
ORIGINAL SERIES COVERS

Curtis King Jr.
PUBLICATION DESIGN

JACK OF FABLES
CREATED BY
Bill Willingham

Logo design by JAMES JEAN

DC Comics, 1700 Broadway, New York, NY 10019
A Warner Bros. Entertainment Company
Printed in the U.S.A. First Printing. ISBN: 978-1-4012-3155-2

Certified Fiber Sourcing
www.sfiprogram.org
Fiber used in this product line meets the sourcing requirements of the SFI program.
www.sfiprogram.org SGS-SFICOC-0130

TABLE OF CONTENTS

DRAMATIS PERSONAE

JACK OF THE TALES

Also known as Little Jack Horner, Jack B. Nimble, Jack the Giant Killer and countless other aliases, this archetypal rogue has descended into literally monstrous complacency.

GARY, THE PATHETIC FALLACY

Formerly one of the most powerful beings on the planet, now reduced to serving as zookeeper for a curmudgeonly dragon.

ROBIN

PRISCILLA

HILLARY

THE PAGE SISTERS

Once the chief librarians for the Fables prison known as the Golden Boughs Retirement Community, these three lovely (and newly mortal) ladies have recently found a new purpose in life.

JACK FROST

Jack's son, a successful adventurer and hero-for-hire celebrated throughout countless worlds.

MACDUFF

Jack Frost's companion and advisor, originally hewn from wood gathered in Geppetto's Sacred Grove.

RAVEN

The famed trickster of Native American legend, now occupied running a roadside attraction with an assortment of fellow Golden Boughs escapees.

WICKED JOHN

Jack's dark-haired alter ego, and the current receptacle of the sword Excalibur.

SAM

A fleet-footed Fable from a politically incorrect era.

BABE

A Walter Mitty-esque blue ox.

THE TINY TERROR OF
TALLER TICKY TOCKY TALES
MAESTRO MOUSE SAVES THE DAY
THE TALENTED TIN MAN OF
RETURN To TREASURE ISLA
FATHER GANDER NURSERY RHY
ADVENTURES of YOUNG MOBY DICK
TICKY TOCKY TIGER TALES
The FOUR LITTLE PIGS
ACRE WOODS MASSA
BOOK
MOBIL

"ARE YOU SURE
IT'S A GOOD IDEA
TO BRING
THE BABY?"

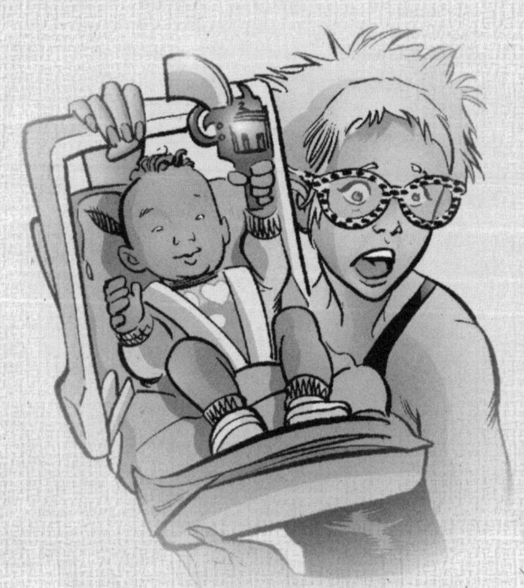

ONE SIDE. STAND ASIDE.

PLEASE.

EVERYONE OUT. **NOW.**

PLEASE.

EXCEPT THE ***STAFF.*** PATRONS GONE. STAFF STAYS, OKAY?

HOT LIBRARIANS!

The First Ingredient in the ULTIMATE JACK OF FABLES STORY!

THAT'S IT--MOVE IT!
THANK YOU.

ARE YOU *SURE* IT'S A GOOD IDEA TO BRING THE BABY, ROBIN?
YOU WANT ME TO *LEAVE HIM ALONE IN THE VAN?*
HE'S A BABY, FOR CHRISSAKES!

BLAM! BLAM!
OKAY, PEOPLE! WE'RE GOING TO MAKE THIS SHORT AND SWEET! DO WHAT WE *SAY* AND NOBODY GETS HURT!

WH-WHAT DO YOU WANT WITH US?
I THINK YOU KNOW *EXACTLY* WHAT WE WANT.

HILLARY! ROBIN! TAKE COVER!

YOU'LL NEVER TAKE HIM ALIVE!
BAM!
BAM! BAM!
QUIET PLEASE!

WE DON'T INTEND TO!
POW!
POW!
DO YOU REALLY EXPECT US TO FALL FOR THE MOUSY LIBRARIAN SHTICK?
AS IF!

TATTA TATTA
TATTA TATTA
TATTA TAT

I INVENTED THE MOUSY LIBRARIAN SHTICK!
BAM!

AUGGH!
KA-POW!

HEY, ASSHOLE! I'M HOLDING A BABY HERE!
BAM!

BAM! TATTA TATTA KA-POW!
NOW, THEN. WHERE WERE WE?
CLICK CLICK CLICK

YOU CAN COME OUT NOW, RICHARDS! I'VE GOT YOUR GIRLFRIEND HERE!

FINE! FINE! JUST PLEASE DON'T HURT HER! HAVEN'T YOU DONE ENOUGH?

NOT NEARLY ENOUGH. NOT YET. WHERE ARE THE BOOKS?
WHAT DO YOU MEAN? THE WHOLE LIBRARY IS FULL OF--

YOU KNOW EXACTLY WHAT BOOKS WE MEAN.

CAN WE MOVE THIS ALONG? SAMMY JUNIOR'S OVERDUE FOR HIS FOUR-O'CLOCK FEEDING.
GAH!
WELL, HILLARY, WHAT'S THE WORD?
THERE'S A *FEW* THINGS OF INTEREST HERE, BUT NOTHING BIG. SEEMS LIKE RICHARDS IS ALL SIZZLE AND NO STEAK.

I DIDN'T KNOW WHAT THOSE BOOKS WERE, I SWEAR IT! I THOUGHT THEY WERE JUST OLD BOOKS!
STANDARD ACQUISITIONS!
YEAH? IS THAT WHY YOU WERE ALL OVER THE INTERNET CLAIMING TO BE THE NEW ***HEAD LIBRARIAN?***

NO! WAIT! I DIDN'T MEAN TO--!
WHO ARE YOU PEOPLE?!
WE'RE THE PAGE SISTERS.
AND ***WE'RE*** THE ONLY LIBRARIANS AROUND HERE.
YOU'RE A POSEUR AND A THIEF. AND WE DON'T TAKE KINDLY TO BOOK THIEVES.
KEEP KIDS READING
BLAM!

WHAT A WASTE. LET'S GO, PRIS.
FUCKING UPSTART SON OF A ***BITCH.***
YOU WANT SOME ***MILKS,*** BOO BOO? HUH? YOU WANT SOME ***MILKIES?***

AT THAT MOMENT...
LOOK OUT, MacDUFF! THERE'S ONE CREEPING UP ON YOUR SIX!
I SEE HIM!
YOU LOOK AFTER YOUR OWN PARTS, JACK, AND DON'T WORRY ABOUT MINE.
ARE YOU STILL HOLDING A GRUDGE ABOUT THAT INCIDENT BACK ON SARUKAN?
DAMMIT, MacDUFF, I SAID I WAS SORRY!
I DIDN'T MEAN TO IMPLY YOU WERE INCOMPETENT THEN, AND I DON'T MEAN IT NOW!
BUT YOU'RE MY FRIEND, AND FRIENDS LOOK OUT FOR EACH OTHER. I'VE HAD YOU AROUND FOR TOO MANY YEARS TO LET ANYTHING HAPPEN TO YOU THIS LATE IN THE GAME!

I THINK WE'VE KILLED ENOUGH OF THEM TO BREAK THE ***BACK*** OF ANY MORE GRAND PLANS OF WORLD CONQUEST.

AGREED.

SO, BACK TO THE SUBJECT. WHAT ***DID*** YOU MEAN WHEN YOU SAID, "THIS LATE IN THE GAME"?

WHAT DO ***YOU*** KNOW THAT I DON'T KNOW?

WE PROMISED EACH OTHER NO MORE ***SECRETS,*** REMEMBER? AFTER THAT NASTY BUSINESS WITH THE GREEN FOG LEAGUE?

ALL I MEANT IS THAT WE'VE BEEN DOING THIS A LONG TIME. WE'VE FOUGHT THE GOOD FIGHT, AND NEARLY ***ALWAYS*** IN THE RIGHT CAUSE.

BUT THERE'LL ALWAYS BE ANOTHER GOOD CAUSE--AN INFINITE NUMBER OF THEM. THEY ***NEVER*** RUN OUT.

SO YOU'RE THINKING--?

AFTER SO MANY YEARS AND SO MANY WORLDS, MAYBE IT'S TIME FOR ***OTHERS*** TO TAKE UP THE NEVER-ENDING STRUGGLE.

MAYBE IT'S TIME TO ***FINALLY*** HANG UP THE FULMINATE BLADE.

LEAVE THE HEROING TRADE?

YES. ***RETIRE,*** TO BE PRECISE.

WE CAN AFFORD IT, RIGHT?

WELL, UH, SURE, I ***GUESS***.

WE HAVE THOSE ACCOUNTS IN THE SHIFTING WORLDS.

AND OUR MINING INVESTMENTS IN THE ALDARA QUOOR ARE STILL RETURNING A DECENT PROFIT.

TRUTH IS, BUDDY, WE COULD RETIRE THIS ***INSTANT*** AND LIVE COMFORTABLY FOR THE REST OF OUR LIVES--NO MATTER HOW LONG THEY TURNED OUT TO BE.

AND NOW WE PAUSE FROM THIS THRILLING MOMENT TO INTRODUCE OUR NEWEST FEATURE...

The hilarious weekly Sunday (mis)adventures of

JACK DRAGON and Gary

The hilarious weekly Sunday (mis)adventures of

JACK DRAGON and Gary

The hilarious weekly Sunday (mis)adventures of

JACK DRAGON and Gary

The hilarious weekly Sunday (mis)adventures of

JACK DRAGON and Gary

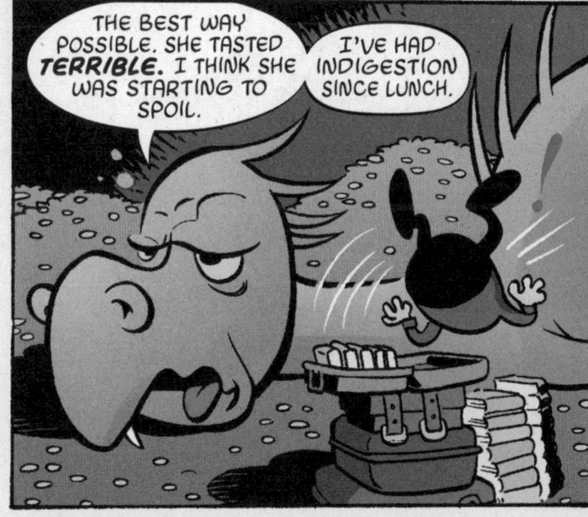

The hilarious weekly Sunday (mis)adventures of

JACK DRAGON and Gary

A BIT LATER...
MacDUFF, DID YOU SEE WHERE MY HAWAIIAN PRINT SHIRT GOT TO?
WHICH ONE? THE YELLOW ONE WITH THE PARROTS, OR THE RED ONE WITH THE PALM TREES?

THE RED ONE.
PUTT PUTT PUTT PUTT PUTT

IT'S STILL IN THE DRYER--ALONG WITH THE YELLOW ONE, TWO PAIRS OF YOUR UNDIES AND ONE SINGLE WHITE SOCK.
PUTT PUTT PUTT PUTT PUTT

IF BOTH SHIRTS ARE TOGETHER, WHY'D YOU NEED TO KNOW WHICH ONE I WAS LOOKING FOR?
BECAUSE I KNEW IT WOULD ANNOY YOU, JACK, AND THAT AMUSES ME.
PUTT PUTT PUTT PUTT PUTT

HURRY UP, MacDUFF. I WANT TO BE PACKED AND CHECKED OUT OF HERE BY NOON--OR WHATEVER PASSES FOR NOON ON THIS WORLD.
THE TRANSPORTATION ENERGIES ARE ALREADY BUILDING UP. WE'LL BE ABLE TO ZAP OURSELVES AWAY FROM HERE SOON.

YOW!
WHO ARE YOU AND HOW'D YOU GET IN HERE?
AM I BY ANY CHANCE ADDRESSING JACK FROST? THE JACK FROST, HERO OF BALTHADOR'S GATE, THE BATTLE OF THE NINE PRINCES IN ONYX, AND WIELDER OF THE FULMINATE BLADE?

UH--SURE.
CAPITAL! MY NAME IS MISTER CLICK. MAVEN OF MESSENGERS. DOYEN OF DOCUMENTARIANS. REGENT OF RECORDERS.

I HAVE A PHONE CALL FOR YOU, SIR.

UH--HELLO?
YEAH, THIS IS JACK FROST. WHO--?

NO, I'M SORRY. I'M NOT IN THE HEROING BUSINESS ANYMORE.
I'M RETIRED.

WHEN? AS OF THIS MORNING, IF YOU MUST KNOW, NOSEY PARKER.
WHO'S THIS, JACK?

I'M MISTER CLICK. HERO OF HISTORIANS. COMMISSAR OF COMMUNICATIONS. BARON OF BROADCAST JOURNALISTS.
SO, NO, AS ATTRACTIVE AS THAT OFFER IS, MacDUFF AND I ARE OUT OF THE MONSTER-KILLING BUSINESS.

HOW DID YOU FIND ME?
YORBIN? SERIOUSLY? NO, HE'S NO LONGER MY AGENT. WE FIRED HIM TWENTY OR THIRTY YEARS AGO, AFTER THE WINTERLANCE FLOATING WORLDS FIASCO.
YOU'D BE THE LEGENDARY MacDUFF, I TAKE IT?

IF HE TOOK ANY MONEY IN MY NAME, YOU GOT SWINDLED. HE'S A SCOUNDREL AND AN ABUSER OF TRUST.
WHY YES, THAT'S ME. SENIOR PARTNER OF MacDUFF AND FROST, HEROIC SERVICES, INC.

A DRAGON?

A REAL LIVE DRAGON, BURNING TOWNS AND VILLAGES, YOU SAY?
NO, IN ALL OUR YEARS IN THE HERO TRADE WE NEVER GOT TO GO UP AGAINST AN ACTUAL DRAGON.

NEW YORK CITY.
OKAY, NOW THE ENTRANCE TO THE REAL LIBRARY IS AROUND HERE SOMEWHERE
THIS BIG NEOCLASSICAL BEHEMOTH IS JUST A DISTRACTION.
HERE, WILL YOU HOLD MY WIDDLE MAN? I'LL HANDLE THIS.
BIG CATS ARE MY THING, AFTER ALL.
ROBIN, YOU GAVE THE BABY A GUN TO PLAY WITH?!
OH, GROW A PAIR, HILLARY. IT'S NOT LIKE IT'S LOADED.
NOW LET ME CONCENTRATE.
HI, KITTY. DIDJA MISS ME?
NO, SORRY, I LEFT MY CHAIR AND WHIP AT HOME, YOU PERVERT.

OH, I THINK YOU KNOW *EXACTLY* WHY WE'RE HERE.
THE ENTRANCE TO THE LIBRARY. THE *REAL* ONE.
CAN WE MOVE THIS ALONG?

PEOPLE ARE STARTING TO STARE.
HOLD YOUR WATER, PRIS. STONE LIONS AREN'T KNOWN FOR THEIR SNAP-TO-IT ATTITUDE.

NO, I WILL *NOT* ANSWER ONE OF YOUR IDIOTIC RIDDLES.
OH, AT AN IMPASSE, ARE WE? TELL YOU WHAT. THERE'S SOME CONSTRUCTION GOING ON DOWN THE STREET. WHY DON'T I GRAB ONE OF THEIR *JACKHAMMERS* AND WE'LL SEE WHAT KIND OF IMPASSE WE'RE AT.

THANK YOU, SWEETIE.

SKRUUUUCH

NOW *THAT'S* MORE LIKE IT.

OKAY, GIRLS. TREAD SOFTLY. WE DON'T KNOW WHAT WE MIGHT RUN UP AGAINST.
OH, COME ON, PRIS. YOU KNOW *EXACTLY* WHAT WE'RE GOING TO RUN UP AGAINST.
WE'RE GOING TO FIND A DUSTY DRY STOREROOM FILLED WITH OLD BOOKS. NONE OF WHICH ARE THE BOOKS WE'RE AFTER.

WE'VE BEEN DOING THIS FOR *YEARS,* AND THE CLOSEST WE'VE EVER COME IS THAT TIME IN TOPEKA WHEN WE FOUND THE READER'S DIGEST VERSION OF *RETURN TO TREASURE ISLAND.* AND EVEN *THAT* TURNED OUT TO BE A FORGERY.

BUCK UP, SIS. OUR BOOKS ARE OUT THERE SOMEWHERE. IT'S JUST A MATTER OF FINDING THEM.
I KNOW, BUT--

BUT NOTHING. WE'RE THE *PAGE SISTERS.* WE'RE THE BIGGEST, BADDEST, HOTTEST LIBRARIANS THE WORLD HAS EVER SEEN.
AND WE *WILL* FIND THOSE BOOKS.

NOW *THIS* IS MORE LIKE IT!

A-GAH!
YOU SAID IT, NIBBLY WIBBLY.

ALL RIGHT, LADIES. SPREAD OUT. LET'S SEE WHAT WE'VE GOT.
OH, WHO ARE WE KIDDING. YOU KNOW IT'S ALL GOING TO BE A BUNCH OF CRAP.

I'VE GOT ABOUT NINE HUNDRED EDWARDIAN FOOT FETISH NOVELS OVER HERE. YOU?
JUST A BUNCH OF NATIONAL GEOGRAPHICS. GRANTED, THEY'RE FROM AN ALTERNATE UNIVERSE, BUT THEY'RE STILL JUST NATIONAL GEOGRAPHICS.
HEY! HEY, LOOK!

I FOUND ONE! THIS IS ONE OF THEM!
GIRLS, I THINK WE ARE FINALLY ON THE RIGHT TRACK!
A REAL BOOK AT LAST!
The FOUR LITTLE PIGS

TODD THE DRAGONSLAYER PREPARES HIMSELF TO GO AGAINST THE MOST DANGEROUS DRAGON HE'S FACED, IN A LONG CAREER OF DRAGON-SLAYING.

HIS ENCHANTED BLADE SCALESPLITTER GLEAMS IN THE SUN. HIS MIGHTY HELM SITS PROUD ON HIS HEAD, AS HE RIDES OFF TO FACE--LET US REITERATE--THE MOST DANGEROUS DRAGON HE HAS EVER FACED.
AND MAKE NO MISTAKE: TODD THE DRAGONSLAYER HAS NEVER FAILED.

NOW, IN THE INTEREST OF FULL DISCLOSURE, TODD HAS NEVER ACTUALLY FACED A DRAGON, LET ALONE SLAIN ONE.
BUT IT'S NOT HIS FAULT! HONEST!

ON THE DAY HE WAS TO FIGHT SNARL THE TERRIBLE, HIS BACK WENT ALL WONKY AGAIN, AND HE HAD TO LIE DOWN.
AND THEN WHEN HE CLIMBED MOUNT DESPAIR TO TACKLE THE BLACK WINDRIDER, IT TURNED OUT THAT HE'D GOTTEN THE DATE WRONG AND THE BLACK WINDRIDER WAS OUT AT A THING.

MAYBE TODD THE DRAGONSLAYER SHOULD SUBCONTRACT THIS ONE DRAGON OUT TO THAT NEW KID, THE ONE WITH THE OWL.
HE'S YOUNG. I'LL BET HE COULD USE THE WORK.

HOW TO SLAY DRAGONS
HOW TO SLAY DRAGONS
BOLLAND

"WHAT KIND OF HEROES WOULD WE BE IF WE RETIRED HAVING NEVER SLAIN AN ACTUAL DRAGON?"

Dragonslayer!

The Second Ingredient in the ULTIMATE JACK OF FABLES STORY!

WE'D QUITE RUN OUT OF OUR CACHE OF MAGICAL LIVING REPLACEMENT WOOD BY THAT TIME. AND I COULDN'T ABIDE NORMAL WOOD PROSTHETICS.
THAT DEAD FEELING IN PLACES-- OH, IT MAKES ME SHIVER JUST TO THINK OF IT.
SO, YOU OBTAINED A GOLDEN BODY SOMEHOW?
NOT YET. NOT BY FAR. YOU HAVE TO CONSIDER, THIS WAS ON A WORLD THAT HAD ONLY THE MOST LIMITED, PRIMITIVE SORTS OF SORCERIES.
THEY COULDN'T DO MIND AND SPIRIT TRANSFERS INTO ANY BUT ALREADY LIVING HOSTS, AND ONLY FAIRLY COMPLEX ANIMAL BIOLOGIES AT THAT.
SPLENDID! ALL DONE! YOU SHINE LIKE A STAR, SQUIRE MacDUFF!
CAPITAL JOB, MR. CLICK. COMMENDABLE.
GETTING BACK TO MY NARRATION--
YES, PLEASE DO. I'M AT THE ACME OF ANTICIPATORY REGARD.
WITH NO POSSIBILITIES OF TRANSFER INTO PLANT LIFE, A NEW WOODEN FORM WAS OUT OF THE QUESTION.
IMAGINE SUCH A BACKWARD CIVILIZATION! IN HINDSIGHT, IT WAS BARELY WORTH SAVING!

IT MUST HAVE PRESENTED YOU WITH A MOST *HELLISH* DILEMMA, SIR.
YOU'VE ***NO*** IDEA!
AND THE WORST PART WAS, MY NEW ***HOST*** HAD TO BE A NEWBORN, SO THERE'D ONLY BE THE MOST RUDIMENTARY CONSCIOUSNESS TO OVER-WRITE.
SO THEY PLOPPED ME INTO A ***PUPPY.***
MY WORD!
A GOD-DAMNED, FLEA-BITTEN, UNHOUSETRAINED PISSING-ALL-OVER-CREATION, ***INCAPABLE-***OF-FLIGHT PUPPY!
I ***LIKED*** THAT PUPPY.
YOU WERE SO ***CUTE*** BACK THEN.

SAYS YOU, JACK! I WAS USELESS AS A PARTNER DURING THAT TIME!
TRUE, BUT THEY PROMISED YOU'D EVENTUALLY GROW BIG AND STRONG AND FULL OF TEETH--IF YOU'D JUST GIVEN IT HALF A CHANCE.

I OBVIOUSLY DISAGREED. AS SOON AS WE COULD, WE HIGH-TAILED IT--LITERALLY IN MY CASE--TO A MORE ADVANCED WORLD, WHERE I WAS TRANSFERRED INTO--
YOUR GOLDEN BODY?
NOT IMMEDIATELY, NO. I WENT BACK TO BEING AN OWL OF COURSE-- I AM WHAT I AM, AFTER ALL.
BUT WE HAD A SURFEIT OF CASH BACK THEN AND WE TRIED-- REMEMBER MY SOLID DIAMOND BODY, JACK? WASN'T THAT MAGNIFICENT?

IF YOU MEAN SO EXPENSIVE IT DROVE US TO THE POOR HOUSE, THEN YES, I DO REMEMBER YOUR DIAMOND PHASE.

TRUE. TURNS OUT THE RIDICULOUS COST WASN'T THE FULL PRICE, BUT JUST THE FIRST PAYMENT OF AN ANNUAL FEE. THE BODY WAS ONLY A RENTAL.

TAUGHT US A LESSON ABOUT ALWAYS READING THE FINE PRINT.
AND TRUTH BE TOLD, IT WASN'T AS AERODYNAMIC AS ONE MIGHT HAVE WISHED. TOO MANY SHARP FACETS. TERRIBLE AIRFLOW. BUT BY THE GODS, I WAS A HANDSOME DEVIL BACK THEN!
SO THEN THE GOLD BODY?
YES, WHEN THE NEXT PAYMENT CAME DUE, AND WE SAW HOW WE'D BEEN HOODWINKED, WE TRADED DOWN TO THE GOLDEN VERSION--WHICH TURNED OUT TO BE THE BETTER ONE ALL ALONG.
VASTLY SUPERIOR FLIGHT CAPABILITIES.
AND THE LASER BEAM EYES TURNED OUT TO BE QUITE HELPFUL, CONSIDERING OUR PROFESSION.
TRUE, TRADING DIAMOND FOR GOLD, WE WERE ABLE TO AFFORD SOME LOVELY UPGRADES.
WHICH ARE GOING TO HELP OUT NICELY IN OUR NEXT MISSION.
NEXT MISSION, JACK? AM I MISTAKEN, OR DIDN'T WE JUST RETIRE?
I'VE DECIDED TO DELAY THAT FOR ONE LAST QUEST, BUDDY. WHAT KINDS OF HEROES WOULD WE BE IF WE RETIRED HAVING NEVER SLAIN AN ACTUAL DRAGON?
HAND ME THE PHONE, MR. CLICK! WE'RE TAKING THE JOB!
HUZZAH!

SAN LUIS OBISPO, CALIFORNIA.
YES, YOUR LITTLE BABY IS DOING JUST **FINEY-WINEY!**
OH, **YES** HE IS!
GET OFF THE **PHONE,** ROBIN. WE'RE ALMOST THERE.
OKAY. PRIS IS SAYING I HAVE TO GO.

OH, WE'RE IN CALIFORNIA. WE HAVE TO GO **ROUGH UP** AN OLD LADY.
OKAY. DON'T WORRY-- I HAVEN'T FOR-GOTTEN.
'BYE, SAM.
SHEATHE YOUR UDDERS, ROBIN. WE'RE **HERE.**

DID YOU **HEAR** SOMETHING, MISTER WIGGLE-BOTTOM?

HELLO, GLADYS WINCHELL. WE'VE BEEN **LOOKING** FOR YOU.

SO WHAT CAN I DO FOR YOU, GIRLS? IS THIS ONE OF THOSE, UM, ENVIRONMENTAL PETITION THINGS, OR--
CUT THE SHIT, LADY. YOU KNOW WHY WE'RE HERE.

I THINK YOU MUST HAVE ME MISTAKEN FOR SOMEONE ELSE. I HONESTLY HAVE NO IDEA--

SEVEN YEARS AGO YOU SOLD THIS BOOK TO A BUYER FROM THE NEW YORK PUBLIC LIBRARY FOR SIXTY THOUSAND DOLLARS.

HE TOLD US THAT YOU'D BEEN DEALING IN BLACK MARKET EXOTIC LIT FOR YEARS, THAT YOU WERE THE ONE TO GO TO FOR--AND I QUOTE-- THE "WEIRD STUFF."
The FOUR LITTLE PIGS

I SUPPOSE IT WAS ONLY A MATTER OF TIME.

IN THOSE DAYS I WAS ALREADY A FAIRLY WELL-KNOWN BROKER OF UNUSUAL OBJETS D'ART.
MY EX-HUSBAND FIRST APPROACHED ME TO HELP HIM SELL A COPY OF THE FURTHER LIFE AND OPINIONS OF TRISTRAM SHANDY, AND WHAT CAN I SAY? IT WAS LOVE AT FIRST SIGHT.

SIX MONTHS AND A FEW DOZEN RARE BOOKS LATER, WE WERE MARRIED.

DID YOU ASK HIM WHERE HE GOT THE BOOKS?
AT FIRST I DID. BUT HE WOULDN'T EVER DISCUSS IT. HE WAS A STRANGE MAN--VERY OPEN, ALMOST GULLIBLE IN SOME WAYS, BUT AT THE SAME TIME, QUITE SECRETIVE.
HE SPENT MOST OF HIS TIME AWAY, EVEN AFTER WE WERE MARRIED, AND HE WAS ALWAYS CAGEY ABOUT WHAT HE WAS DOING, AND WHO HE WAS DOING IT WITH.

DIDN'T THAT SEEM STRANGE TO YOU? WEREN'T YOU SUSPICIOUS?

OF COURSE I WAS SUSPICIOUS. YOU'RE TOO YOUNG TO UNDERSTAND THIS, DEAR, BUT WHEN A WOMAN GETS TO BE A CERTAIN AGE...WELL, YOU LEARN TO LOOK THE OTHER WAY IF YOU HAVE TO.

I WAS IN LOVE, YOU SEE.
COME ON. I'LL SHOW YOU WHAT YOU CAME FOR.

IT WAS GREAT WHILE IT LASTED. BUT THEN THINGS STARTED GETTING WEIRD. I MEAN, REALLY WEIRD.
IT WAS THE COWS THAT FINALLY DID IT. THAT'S WHERE I DREW THE LINE.

I'M SORRY. DID YOU SAY "COWS"?
IN THE BEGINNING, MY EX-HUSBAND WAS MORE THAN HAPPY TO TAKE CASH IN PAYMENT FOR THE BOOKS. NO WIRE TRANSFERS OR CASHIER'S CHECKS. ONLY CASH.

BUT AFTER A WHILE, HE SEEMED TO BE GETTING ANXIOUS. HE WAS GONE MORE AND MORE OFTEN. IN HIS SLEEP, HE'D MOAN, "NEVER ENOUGH! NEVER ENOUGH! NO MATTER WHAT I DO IT'S NEVER ENOUGH!"

HE STARTED ASKING FOR TANGIBLE THINGS IN EXCHANGE FOR THE BOOKS, LIKE GOLD, DIAMONDS, PRECIOUS STONES, THAT SORT OF THING. AND THAT WAS STRANGE, BUT...
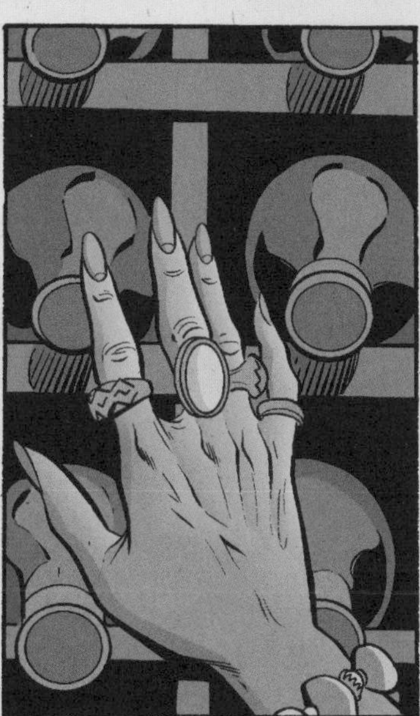

THEN HE STARTED ASKING FOR COWS.
CRUNK

YES. HE SAID HE DIDN'T HAVE TIME FOR MIDDLEMEN ANY-MORE...
COWS.
...AND THAT IF I WANTED TO KEEP HIM AROUND I HAD TO START GIVING HIM...COWS. AND I KNOW FOR A FACT, LADIES--

--HE WAS NO RANCHER.

MS. WINCHELL, DO YOU HAVE ANY IDEA WHERE WE CAN FIND YOUR EX-HUSBAND?

I CAN GIVE YOU THE NAME OF THE TOWN, BUT THAT'S ALL.

I WARN YOU, THOUGH. I DON'T THINK IT'S ANYPLACE NORMAL.
I THINK THIS PLACE IS... SOMEWHERE OTHER.

AH. WELL, THAT IS OTHER, ALL RIGHT.
JESUS, PRIS, DO YOU KNOW WHERE THIS IS?
I'VE HEARD OF IT, YES.

HERE THEY ALL ARE. ALL I HAVE LEFT.
CLICK

THERE'S THE FOURTH AND FIFTH JUNGLE BOOKS, AN ILLUSTRATED SNOW WHITE AND THE THIRTEEN DWARVES, AND OF COURSE ALICE'S ADVENTURES BEYOND THE GRAVE.

YOU UNDERSTAND THAT WE HAVE TO TAKE THESE BOOKS, DON'T YOU?
YES. I DO.

GO, THEN. TAKE THE BOOKS. ALL I ASK IN RETURN IS THAT WHEN YOU FIND HIM, YOU FIGURE IT OUT AND THEN YOU COME TELL ME.
TELL YOU WHAT?
TELL ME WHAT HE DID WITH THE COWS! IT'S KILLING ME NOT KNOWING!

MS. WINCHELL, WHAT WAS YOUR HUSBAND'S NAME?
HIS NAME? I THOUGHT YOU KNEW.

MY HUSBAND'S NAME WAS GARY.

YERMO, CALIFORNIA.
POPULATION: TIRED, DUSTY, GETTING OLD, AND PLUMB WORN OUT BY THE DESERT SUN.
MAYBE YOU GIRLS CAN TRY TO STOP BY, SEEING AS HOW YOU'RE ALMOST IN THE NEIGHBORHOOD?

WINDING THE CLOCK BACK AN HOUR OR TWO...
OKAY, IF YOU'VE GOT A SCHEDULE, I UNDERSTAND. BUSY DAYS, HUH?
YERMO ELECTRICAL, PLUMBING AND AIR CONDITIONING.

TELL THE LITTLE SQUIRT-PANTS I LOVE HIM, AND DON'T FORGET, IT'S MY WEEK-END.
'BYE NOW. TAKE CARE.
1987

SORRY ABOUT THAT, MR. BROOK. I KNOW YOU DON'T WANT THE BUSINESS LINE TIED UP.
OH, THAT'S OKAY, SAM. ONE CALL EVERY BLUE MOON ISN'T EXACTLY A HARDSHIP.

I'LL GET BACK TO IT NOW--TRY TO BANG A LITTLE MORE LIFE INTO MRS. ALBRIGHT'S *ANCIENT* BOILER.
YOU WERE A BETTER SALESMAN, BOSS, YOU COULD TALK HER INTO *FINALLY* BUYING A NEW ONE.

IF I WAS A BETTER SALESMAN, I WOULDN'T BE *STUCK* IN THIS PISSANT TOWN, WEARING MY YEARS AWAY.
SPEAKING OF WHICH, SAM, HOW *LONG* HAVE YOU BEEN HERE?

A SPELL.
QUITE A SPELL, YOU MEAN. YOU WERE HERE WHEN MY *DAD* RAN THE BUSINESS, AND YOU WERE OLD AS THE HILLS THEN.

HOW OLD *ARE* YOU, SAM?

I BEEN DOWN A FEW ROADS IN MY TIME. NOT INCLINED TO SAY *MORE* ON THE SUBJECT.

I'LL GET BACK TO WORK NOW.

NATASHA BLATZKY HAS LANDED HER BIGGEST PART YET. IT'S THE ROLE OF CHEERLEADER NUMBER THREE IN AN EPISODE OF THE EMMY-NOMINATED *CRIME SCENE: BARSTOW!*
ON AIR

NATASHA HAS, OF COURSE, DONE SOME ***SERIOUS*** CHARACTER WORK--SHE'S NOT ONE TO COME TO THE SET UNPREPARED.
SHE'S DEVELOPED AN ELABORATE BACKSTORY FOR CHEERLEADER NUMBER THREE WHICH, SADLY, THE NARRATIVE DOESN'T GIVE HER MUCH ***ROOM*** TO EXPLORE.
ON AIR

BUT THAT'S WHAT ***ACTING*** IS ALL ABOUT. DURING HER BIG SCENE, SHE SNAPS HER GUM IN A WAY THAT ONLY A RUSSIAN SPY ***POSING*** AS A CHEERLEADER COULD SNAP.
AND WHEN SHE SAYS, "OH, MY GOD!" WHAT SHE'S ***REALLY*** SAYING IS THAT SHE MISSES HER CHILDHOOD IN THE TUNDRA OF KAMCHATKA, HARSH THOUGH IT WAS.
ON AIR

BUT IT'S NOT UNTIL CHEERLEADER NUMBER THREE FLIPS HER POM-POMS ***JUST SO*** THAT WE REALIZE THE TRUTH--
--THAT THIS RUSSIAN SPY IS MERELY ***POSING*** AS A CHEERLEADER AS RESEARCH FOR HER ROLE AS CHEERLEADER NUMBER TWO IN AN UPCOMING EPISODE OF *CRIME SCENE: DAYTON!*
ON AIR

ON AIR

TURNS OUT THAT RUSSIAN SPYING DOESN'T PAY ALL THAT WELL, AFTER ALL--***DESPITE*** WHAT IT SAYS IN THE BROCHURE.
ON AIR

ROUTE 66
CAN'T WE JUST DRIVE STRAIGHT TO GRANDMA'S?

I'M SICK OF BEING IN THE CAR!
ME TOO!
WHAT, AND MISS OUT ON THE DINO DINER AND ASSORTED ATTRACTIONS? ARE YOU KIDS CRAZY?

MOM! TELL LUKE TO STOP TOUCHING ME!
I DON'T KNOW, AUBREY. WE'VE BEEN COMING HERE EVERY YEAR FOR THE PAST TEN YEARS. MAYBE WE COULD GIVE IT A PASS JUST THIS ONCE?

YOU KNOW, WHEN I MET YOU, YOU WERE NOTHING BUT A DEPARTMENT STORE MANNEQUIN WHO'D BEEN BROUGHT TO LIFE IN A SERIES OF MISHAPS! YOU'D BE NOTHING WITHOUT ME!
OH, AGAIN WITH THE MANNEQUIN BUSINESS. YOU'RE JUST LUCKY I WAS NAÏVE ENOUGH BACK THEN TO FALL FOR A NERD LIKE YOU.

STOP FIGHTING! YOU'RE GOING TO GIVE ME AN EATING DISORDER! I SWEAR!

OH, NOW YOU'VE DONE IT. EOWYN'S GETTING AN EATING DISORDER.
I WISH YOU'D LISTEN TO THE THERAPIST WHEN SHE SAYS--

AH, BUT THE POINT IS MOOT, NOELLE.
WE'RE HERE!

KANSAS TWISTER!
DINO DINER
LOT A
OH, JOY.

WELCOME TO DINO DINER AND ASSORTED ATTRACTIONS, THE HAPPIEST, MOST HAPPENIN' PLACE ON ROUTE SIXTY-SIX. HOW MANY?
FOUR, PLEASE.

BAKER, MY MAN, HOW THE HELL DID WE END UP ON TICKET DUTY AGAIN? I TELL YOU, IF REVISE SHOWED UP AND OFFERED TO TAKE ME BACK TO THE GOLDEN BOUGHS, I'D GO WILLINGLY.
THE HELL YOU SAY. THIS IS GOOD, HONEST WORK. WORK A MAN CAN BE PROUD OF.
LIKE BAKING, FOR INSTANCE. NOTHING WRONG WITH BAKING.

AND I ALSO WANT A HAM MELT WITH CHEDDAR CHEESE AND MAYO AND EXTRA BACON AND CURLY FRIES AND A COKE AND I ALSO WANT A FRIED PEANUT BUTTER, BACON AND BANANA SANDWICH WITH THE POWDERED SUGAR ON THE SIDE AND EXTRA BACON AND SWEET POTATO NIBBLES AND A DIET COKE AND I ALSO WANT AN ORDER OF CHILI CHEESE FRIES WITH A SMALL SALAD.
AND A SIDE ORDER OF BACON.
YOU WANT GRAVY ON THE FRIES, SIR?

WE'RE STILL LIVING THE DREAM. RIGHT, RAVEN?
I MEAN, WE ARE, AREN'T WE?
ARE YOU KIDDING, KEMOSABE? LOOK AROUND YOU! WHEN WE CAME HERE THIS PLACE WAS NOTHING, A MUNDY CRAPHOLE.
AND NOW LOOK AT IT. WE'VE BUILT THIS PLACE UP INTO SOMETHING UNIQUE! SOMETHING BOLD! SOMETHING, DARE I SAY... FABLEWORTHY!

OH, ISN'T HE MARVELOUS? HAVE YOU EVER SEEN SUCH A THING?
OBVIOUSLY IT'S A MIDGET IN A PIG SUIT. I MEAN, COME ON. REAL PIGS DON'T HAVE MOVES LIKE THAT.
COUGH COUGH DOUCHE-WAFFLE COUGH COUGH
10

ACTUALLY, MOTHER GOOSE WASN'T REALLY A GOOSE. THAT WAS JUST HER NAME.
DO YOU KIDS WANT TO GO HEAR A STORY?
MO-OM!
AND THEN OFFICER McCLANE CAUGHT THE MILLEN-NIUM FALCON IN AN INTERNET!
10

THIS IS ALL DONE WITH ANIMATRONICS, RIGHT? ANIMATRONICS AND CGI. PROBABLY LASERS TOO, AM I RIGHT?
NOPE, WE'RE ALL REAL. COMPLETELY REAL. IT'S JUST THAT THERE'S A MAGIC SPELL ON THE PLACE THAT CONVINCES YOU IT'S ALL FAKE.

RIGHT. HOLOGRAMS. THAT'S WHAT I THOUGHT.

JUST A BUNCH OF CHEAP TRICKS.
COME ON, DAD! LET'S GO!

OKAY, LET'S GO THEN. ISN'T THIS PLACE GREAT?
WOULD THAT I COULD SO READILY DEPART THIS PLACE!
EMPLO ONLY

IF YOU REALLY WANT TO LEAVE, THERE'S A FEW OF US WHO'D JOIN YOU. WE COULD TRY TO FIX UP THE OL' BUS, FINALLY HEAD OFF TO FABLETOWN.
NO, DEAR BOY. FABLETOWN IS A MYTH, NOTHING MORE. JUST A STORY WE TOLD BACK IN THE GOLDEN BOUGHS TO KEEP OUR HOPES UP.

NO, IT'S NOT A MYTH. IT WAS REAL, BUT IT WAS DESTROYED YEARS AGO.
I HEARD IT WAS SOMEWHERE OUTSIDE FRESNO.
I'M AFRAID BOTH OF YOU ARE UNDER A DELUSION. THERE'S NO FABLETOWN TODAY NOR WAS THERE EVER ONE.

THAT'S A LIE! REMEMBER WHEN JACK HORNER WAS HERE, WAY BACK WHEN? HE TOLD US HE CAME FROM FABLETOWN. IT HAS TO BE REAL!

JACK HORNER? THAT SCALAWAG?
EVERYTHING JACK HORNER EVER TOLD YOU IS A LIE.

The hilarious weekly Sunday (mis)adventures of

JACK DRAGON and Gary

The hilarious weekly Sunday (mis)adventures of

JACK DRAGON and Gary

SOMEONE'S COMING, GARY. A SHADOWED MAN, COMING TO KILL ME AND TAKE MY TREASURE HOARD.
I KNOW, JACK. I CAN FEEL IT, TOO. LIKE THE END IS ON ITS WAY.

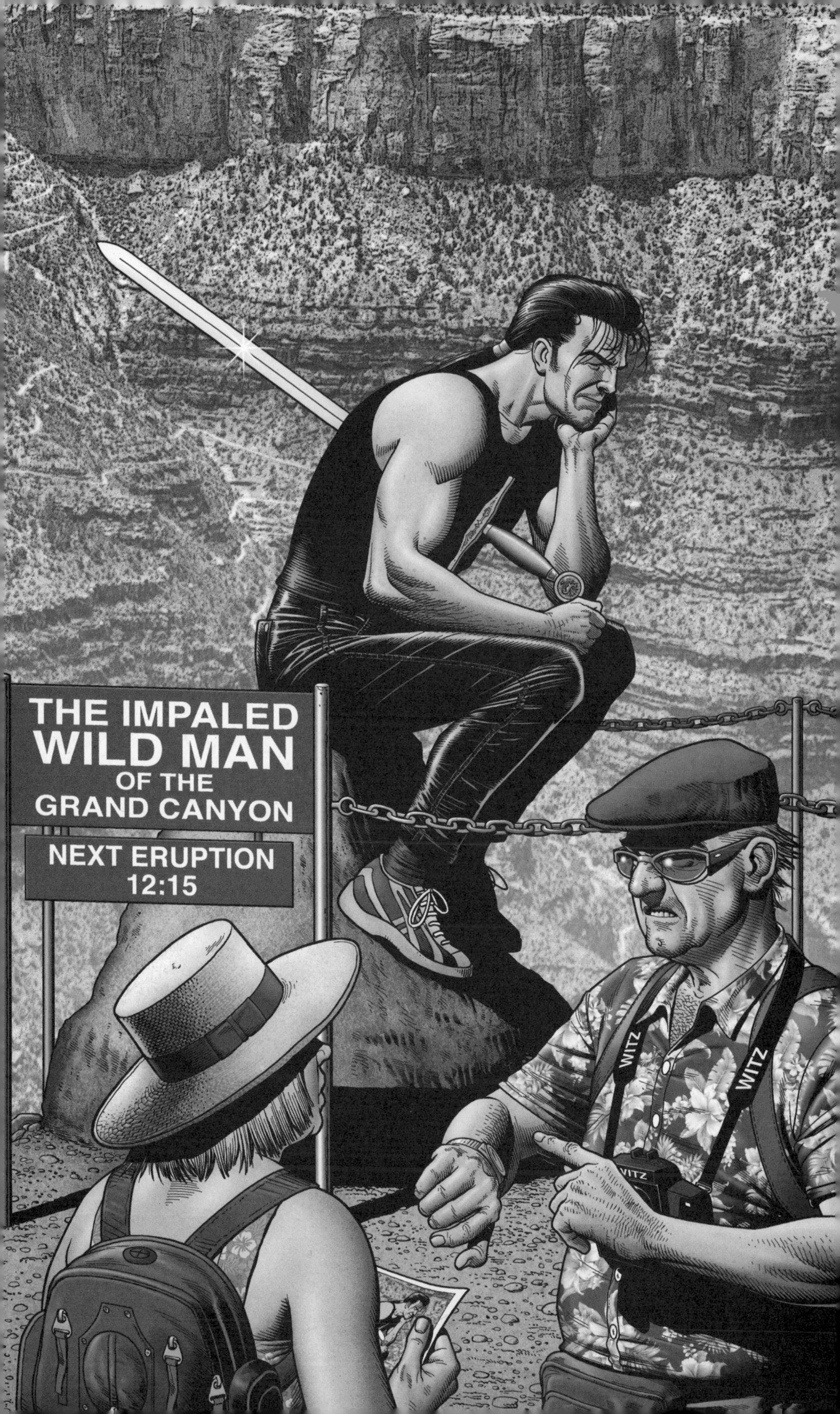
THE IMPALED WILD MAN OF THE GRAND CANYON
NEXT ERUPTION 12:15
WITZ
WITZ
WITZ

"LATELY
I WONDER
IF MY LIFE
HASN'T BECOME
SOME KIND OF
HIDEOUS PARODY."

THE IMPALED WILD MAN!

HE THIRD INGREDIENT IN THE MOST UNABASHEDLY GENIUS JACK OF FABLES STORY IN HUMAN HISTORY!

WE DON'T NEED TO BUY FILM NO MORE, MAMA. I KEEP TELLING YOU. WE GOT THE *DIGITAL* NOW.
TRAM RIDES:
$37 PER PERSON ROUND TRIP
THE Impaled
of

THE INCREDIBLE, IMPOSSIBLE
IMPALED WILD MAN
GRAND CANYON!
THIS IS GOING TO BE GREAT, AUBREY! YOU'LL FORGET ABOUT NOELLE AND THE KIDS LEAVING YOU IN NO TIME!
YEAH, I GUESS, MIKEY. BUT I STILL SAY WE SHOULD'VE GONE BACK TO VEGAS AGAIN.
IMPALED WILD MAN

THERE HE IS, MAMA! OVER *THERE!*
THE WILD MAN!
OH, MY! HE'S SO--
--*SAVAGE!*
CAUTION!
DANGER! STAY BACK!
YOU'RE HERE!
YOU'VE FINALLY MADE IT!
THIS IS THE WILD MAN!

WOW! HE *REALLY* STINKS! THAT'S REALLY CLEVER OF THEM. ADDS TO THE SENSE OF AUTHENTICITY.
THE SWORD LOOKS *FAKE,* THOUGH.

TAKE MY PICTURE WITH HIM, MAMA!
SIR, YOU AREN'T *ALLOWED* TO APPROACH THE--
PLEASE USE CAUTION!

LOOKIE HERE! LOOK AT ME!
I CAPTURED THE FAMOUS WILD MAN!
SIR!
PLEASE USE CAUTION!
DANGER! STAY BACK!

BETTER YET! TAKE A PICTURE OF THIS, MAMA!
I'M GOING TO PULL THE SWORD OUT OF THE SAVAGE!

I'M LIKE KING ARTHUR!
TAKE THE PICTURE, MAMA! TAKE THE PICTURE!
SIR! YOU CAN'T DO THAT!
WHAT THE HELL?!

WOW. THIS THING IS REALLY STUCK IN THERE.
MUST BE ATTACHED TO SOME KIND OF HARNESS, RIGHT?
DON'T BREAK THE EXHIBIT, PAPA!
THAT'S IT!

I'VE HAD ALL I CAN STAND!
POW!

DANGER!
E USE
TION!
AND I CAN'T STAND NO MORE!
DO NO
APPRO
You BELIEVE
HIS IS
E WILD
MAN!
OU'VE
FINALLY
MADE IT!

GET BACK! GET BACK, EVERYONE! THE WILD MAN IS ESCAPING!
PLEASE U
UTION

HOLD IT! I'LL SHOOT!
WILL YOU? WILL YOU, HYRAM?
YOU'VE FINALLY MADE IT!

GO AHEAD!

GO AHEAD AND SHOOT ALL YOU WANT, PAL!
SPLORCHH

RATTLE-
TINK-
RATTLE-
TINK

PEMBINA, NORTH DAKOTA.
HE'S LATE.
HE'S MAYBE FOUR SECONDS LATE, PRISCILLA. HE'S COMING ALL THE WAY FROM YERMO, CALIFORNIA, TO MEET US, YOU KNOW.
MOBILE

EVERY SECOND WE WAIT IS ONE MORE SECOND WE'RE NOT USING TO REBUILD THE GREAT LIBRARY.
WE'VE BEEN WORKING ON THIS FOR YEARS. DECADES. A COUPLE EXTRA MINUTES AREN'T GOING TO MAKE ANY DIFFERENCE.
I KNOW, I KNOW. IT'S JUST THAT WE'RE SO--

--CLOSE.
HEY, THERE.
MOBIL
SORRY I'M LATE. I GOT CAUGHT UP TANGLING WITH AN ANGRY A.C. COMPRESSOR.

HOW'S MY LITTLE SQUIRT-PANTS, HUH? YOU READY TO SPEND SOME QUALITY TIME WITH THE OLD MAN?
I WROTE DOWN EVERYTHING YOU NEED TO KNOW, WHEN THE FEEDINGS ARE, NAPTIMES, ET CETERA.
OH, AND DON'T FORGET HIS STUFFED TIGER.

OF COURSE NOT. WHAT'S THE TIGER'S NAME?
BUTTER.
NATURALLY. SHOULD HAVE GUESSED THAT MY OWN SELF.

WELL, IT'S ABOUT DAMN TIME. I CAN ALMOST SMELL THOSE BOOKS. IT'S LIKE THEY'RE CALLING OUT TO ME.
WITH ANY LUCK, WE'LL REACH OUR DESTINATION SOME TIME TOMORROW.

SO, ROBIN, I HAVE TO ASK. YOU AND SAM? I JUST DON'T SEE IT.
WELL, YOU KNOW, IT WAS JUST A ONE-NIGHT THING.

I KNOW HE'S NOT MUCH TO LOOK AT, BUT HE'S INCREDIBLY SPRY FOR A GUY HIS AGE.

AND ALTHOUGH HE MAY BE QUITE FAST IN SOME WAYS, HE DEFINITELY KNOWS HOW TO TAKE HIS TIME IN OTHERS.
IF YOU CATCH MY DRIFT.

MUST WE? MUST WE CATCH YOUR DRIFT? 'CAUSE I JUST WANT TO DRIVE.
BOOK MOBILE
U.S.-CANADI
BORDER

THAT'S FIVE HAMSTERS TO YOU, YOUR HOLINESS.
I SEE YOUR FIVE HAMSTERS AND I FOLD.
I HAVE A DEGREE IN THINKING FROM THE UNIVERSE OF HISTORY.
BEHOLD!
I DON'T KNOW HOW TO PLAY THIS HAND.
HEY, RAVEN! OVER HERE!
BIRD SPIRIT! WHAT UP, DUDE? WE'RE PLAYING CARDS.
NO, YOU'RE NOT. THIS IS A DREAM.
THAT SUCKS. I THINK I WAS WINNING. I HAD THE G OF HORSE-SHOES.
DO YOU REALIZE HOW STUPID YOU SOUND?
NOW, PAY ATTENTION--I HAVE A LOT TO TELL YOU, AND R.E.M. SLEEP ONLY LASTS FOR A COUPLE OF MINUTES.

OKAY, SO WHAT'S **SO** IMPORTANT?
YOU'VE BEEN SCREWING UP BAD, DUMBASS, AND I'VE COME TO **SET YOU** ON THE RIGHT PATH.
OH, AND YOU MIGHT WANT TO **CHANGE** INTO YOUR BIRD FORM FOR THIS.
HUH? HOW COME?
WHOA!
YOU **SUCK!**
I WARNED YOU.
SEE WHAT I MEAN? YOU'VE GONE **SOFT.** YOU FORGOT YOUR **PURPOSE.** AND NOW YOU'RE WASTING YOUR LIFE FLIPPING BURGERS AT A ROADSIDE ATTRACTION.

--IS TO PROTECT JACK HORNER.
AND YOU'VE CLEARLY BEEN DOING A MISERABLE JOB.
WOW, YOU'RE RIGHT-- I COMPLETELY FORGOT ABOUT THAT.

HOLY SHIT! IS HE BEING HELD PRISONER IN THERE OR SOMETHING?
UM...YEAH. IN A MANNER OF SPEAKING.
BUT HERE'S THE THING. A VAST ARRAY OF NASTY THINGS IS COMING TO KILL HIM. THEY ALL WANT HIM DEAD, FOR ONE REASON OR ANOTHER.

WHAT DO YOU EXPECT ME TO DO? I'M JUST A HUMBLE FRY COOK!
NO, YOU'RE NOT! YOU'RE RAVEN, THE GREATEST TRICKSTER THAT EVER WAS, AND WHAT I EXPECT YOU TO DO IS GATHER TOGETHER EVERY ALLY YOU CAN MUSTER AND COME HERE TO SAVE JACK HORNER!

WHERE IS THIS PLACE?
THE OLD ONES CALLED IT THE STRAITS OF MANITOU. THAT'S WHERE YOU HAVE TO GO. THAT'S WHERE YOU HAVE TO MAKE YOUR STAND. GOT IT?

GRRRRRR!

I GOT IT! I GOT IT.

SO WHAT'S THIS BIG MEETING ALL ABOUT?
WHO CARES? I'M SO SICK OF THIS PLACE I COULD EAT SOMEONE.
DINO DINER

YOU THINK DOROTHY HAD THE RIGHT IDEA ALL THOSE YEARS AGO? STRIKING OFF ON HER OWN? MAYBE WE SHOULD HAVE GONE WITH HER.

MMM, YES AND NO. IF YOU'LL RECALL, SHE WAS ACTING PRETTY WEIRD AROUND THE TIME SHE LEFT, ONCE WE GOT ALL OUR MEMORIES BACK.
SHE GOT ALL, YOU KNOW... DARK.

HUH. COME TO THINK OF IT, DOROTHY ALWAYS WAS KIND OF CREEPY, WASN'T SHE?

THIS MEETING BETTER NOT BE ABOUT VOMIT DETAIL ON THE TILT-A-WHIRL. I SAID I'D MAUL THE NEXT S.O.B. THAT ASKED ME TO DO IT, AND I WAS SERIOUS.
LISTEN UP, FOLKS! I HEREBY CALL THIS EMERGENCY STAFF MEETING TO ORDER!

WHEN WE FIRST CAME HERE ALL THOSE YEARS AGO, AFTER THE DESTRUCTION OF THE GOLDEN BOUGHS, WE SAID THAT THIS WAS ONLY A *TEMPORARY* HOME, RIGHT? WE ALWAYS KNEW THERE WERE BIGGER AND BETTER THINGS OUT THERE WAITING FOR US.
SO I ASK YOU, ***WHAT HAPPENED?*** WE DESERVE BETTER THAN TO BE STUCK HERE IN THE MIDDLE OF ***NOWHERE,*** FLIPPING BURGERS AND OTHER GRILLED CUTS OF MEAT.
WHAT HAPPENED TO OUR ***PRIDE?*** WHAT HAPPENED TO OUR ***NOBILITY?***
ARE WE ***FABLES?*** OR ARE WE JUST A BUNCH OF STUPID ***MUNDYS?***
HEAR, HEAR!

WHAT EXACTLY ARE YOU TRYING TO SAY, DEAR BOY? AREN'T YOU THE ONE WHO'S ALWAYS GOING ON ABOUT HONEST WORK? ABOUT BUILDING SOMETHING HERE, SOMETHING UNIQUE AND BOLD?
OH, THAT? FUCK THAT.
I'M TALKING ABOUT SOMETHING IMPORTANT HERE! I'M TALKING ABOUT THE BIG DREAM!

RAVEN, ARE YOU SAYING WHAT I THINK YOU'RE SAYING? ARE YOU TALKING ABOUT--

THAT'S RIGHT, BUTCHER! I'M TALKING ABOUT FABLETOWN!

FABLETOWN? BALDERDASH! IT'S A FOOL'S ERRAND! I'VE SAID IT BEFORE AND I'LL SAY IT AGAIN. THERE IS NO FABLETOWN!
EXIT

NOT ONLY DOES FABLETOWN EXIST, MY OYSTER-SWILLING FRIEND, BUT I KNOW EXACTLY WHERE IT IS.

MY BIRD SPIRIT CAME TO ME IN A DREAM! HE SHOWED ME THE WAY TO FABLETOWN! HE SAID THAT I HAD BEEN CHOSEN TO LEAD YOU ALL THERE!
HE TOLD ME THAT THE PLACE IS FULL OF BEAUTIFUL WOMEN, HAND-SOME MEN, AND HEALTHY ANIMALS!

PUNF
PUNF
PUNF

THERE'S BREAKFAST IN BED IN FABLETOWN! YOU CAN SPEND YOUR DAYS DOING WHATEVER YOU LIKE, AND THERE'S A PARTY EVERY NIGHT. WITH LIVE MUSIC!

SHISH
SHISH

MY FRIENDS, THERE IS A BUS RIGHT OUTSIDE THAT'S WAITING TO TAKE US THERE. WE CAN LEAVE RIGHT NOW.
WHO'S WITH ME?!

CRICK
CRICK
CRICK

HUZZAH!
FABLE-TOWN HERE WE COME!

WE JUST HAVE TO MAKE ONE TINY LITTLE STOP FIRST...
JESUS, WHAT A TRAIN WRECK THIS IS GOING TO BE!
I LOVE MY JOB!

FULMINATE BLADE?
CHECK.
RUBY RAY?
CHECK.

ARE YOU ABSOLUTELY *CERTAIN* YOU WON'T AGREE TO HAVE ME ALONG TO DOCUMENT YOUR BATTLE WITH THE DRAGON?
IF IT'S *QUALITY* YOU'RE WORRIED ABOUT, I CAN PROVIDE YOU WITH A LIST OF VERY SATISFIED CUSTOMERS, INCLUDING THE QUEEN OF ANTRIGONET, AND THE MARCH WYRM OF PLANET SEVENTY-TWO.

ALTHOUGH, IN THE INTEREST OF FULL DISCLOSURE, IF YOU MEET A FAIR MAIDEN ON THIS QUEST AND *CHOOSE* TO MARRY HER, THEN I'LL HAVE TO BOW OUT, BECAUSE I DON'T *DO* WEDDINGS.
SORRY, MISTER CLICK. MacDUFF AND I PREFER TO GO IT ***ALONE.*** IT'S JUST HOW WE OPERATE.

BUT THANKS FOR ALL YOUR HELP.

IN THAT CASE, IT HAS BEEN AN HONOR TO KNOW THE TWO OF YOU. AND I PRAY YOU FIND YOUR FINAL QUEST TO BE BOTH EXHILARATING AND SUCCESSFUL BEYOND MEASURE.
MUCH OBLIGED, MISTER CLICK.
NEXT STOP, THE MYSTICAL LAND OF ***MAWN ITO BAH--*** TO FACE A ***DRAGON!***

WE'VE ARRIVED.

JACK, WAIT.
WHAT IF WE'RE MAKING A MISTAKE?

WHAT ARE YOU TALKING ABOUT, OLD CHUM? YOU'VE NEVER BACKED DOWN FROM A FIGHT BEFORE.
IT'S JUST THAT WE'VE GOT ALL THE RICHES WE COULD EVER WANT. WE'RE LEGENDS ON WORLDS BEYOND NUMBER. WE'VE SAVED THE DAY ON SO MANY DAYS I'VE LOST COUNT.
MAYBE IT'S TIME FOR US TO BOW OUT GRACEFULLY. MAYBE THIS IS SOMEONE ELSE'S DRAGON TO SLAY.

I UNDERSTAND WHAT YOU'RE SAYING, OLD FRIEND. BUT WE'RE HERE NOW, AND IT'LL BE DAYS BEFORE WE CAN TRAVEL TO ANOTHER WORLD ANYWAY.
THERE'S A RUTHLESS DRAGON SOMEWHERE OUT HERE, AND I CAN'T JUST STAND IDLY BY WHILE IT PREYS ON THIS LAND, NO MATTER HOW REMOTE OR SEEMINGLY UNIMPORTANT IT MIGHT BE.

SO WHAT DO YOU SAY, MacDUFF?
ARE WE GOING TO SLAY THIS DRAGON, OR WHAT?

JACK? JACK?
ARE YOU AWAKE?

DID YOU FEEL IT, TOO?
I DID. THE SHADOWED MAN IS SUDDENLY VERY CLOSE, I'M AFRAID.

LATELY I WONDER IF IT'S ALL WORTH IT, IF MY LIFE HASN'T BE-COME SOME KIND OF HIDEOUS PARODY.
AND I HAVE TO ROLL AROUND IN MY TREASURE FOR LONGER AND LONGER EACH TIME TO STOP FEELING THAT WAY.

BUT THAT'S NOT ALL, GARY. I'VE BEEN HAVING VISIONS. DIRE OMENS.
THEY'RE INDISTINCT AND HAZY, BUT THEY'RE TRUE. I CAN SENSE IT.

TELL ME WHAT YOU SEE, JACK.

"I SEE A WILD MAN, A HIRSUTE BEAST MADE OF EQUAL PARTS FURY AND VENGEANCE.
"AND I SEE THREE SISTERS, ONCE IMBUED WITH A GREAT COSMIC POWER, NOW MERELY HUMAN BUT NO LESS DEADLY.
"AND I GET THE DISTINCT SENSE THAT I'VE BONED ALL THREE OF THEM.

"I SEE A RAGTAG BUNCH OF FABLES, COME TO FIGHT BY BY SIDE, MY ONLY ALLIES IN THE COMING BATTLE.
"AND MOST TERRIFYING OF ALL, I SEE THE SHADOWED MAN AND HIS WINGED FAMILIAR, COME TO SLASH AT ME WITH A BLADE OF FIRE. BUT WHEN I TRY TO GET A GLIMPSE OF HIS FACE, I SEE ONLY MY OWN STARING BACK AT ME.
"OH, AND I SEE SOME MOUNTIES, TOO. BUT I THINK THEY'RE MAINLY CANNON FODDER."
IS THIS IT, JACK? IS THIS THE END?
IT MAY BE, PALOMINO. IT JUST MAY BE.

IT JUST SO HAPPENS THAT I, OMAR KNORR, M.D., AM THE NEXT-TO-WORST DOCTOR IN AMERICA. THIS IS NO MERE VALUE JUDGMENT. THERE'S CONCRETE PROOF.

TO WIT: I GRADUATED FOUR HUNDRED AND SIXTH IN A CLASS OF FOUR HUNDRED AND SEVEN--
--FROM THE LOWEST-RANKED MEDICAL SCHOOL IN THE UNITED STATES STILL IN OPERATION: THE HOBOKEN COLLEGE OF MEDICINE AND CULINARY ARTS.

AND WHILE I MAY NOT BE THE WORST DOCTOR IN AMERICA, I'M STILL PRETTY BAD.
FOR ONE THING, I TEND TO FAINT AT THE SIGHT OF BLOOD. A LOT OF TIMES I FORGET WHICH MEDICINES DO WHAT.
HECK, I DON'T EVEN KNOW WHAT A SPLEEN IS.

ONE TIME, IN MY SURGICAL ROTATION, I ACCIDENTALLY LEFT A PIECE OF CHEESE IN A GUY'S ABDOMEN. NO LIE. THERE WAS A BIG LAWSUIT AND EVERYTHING.

BUT WHENEVER I START TO FEEL DOWN ABOUT MYSELF, I JUST REMEMBER GOOD OL' NUMBER 407, STENNY KEMP.
GOD, WHAT A LOSER THAT GUY TURNED OUT TO BE!

BOLLAND
JACK OF FABLES 31

"WHAT KIND OF TWILIGHT ZONE WACKYVILLE HAVE WE STUMBLED INTO?"

SOMEWHERE UP NORTH.
THAT OUGHTTA DO IT.

THERE YOU ARE, OLD BUDDY! I THOUGHT I'D LOST YOU FOR GOOD!
YOU'RE A TRUE FRIEND, BARRY, AND THAT'S A FACT.

YOU'RE RIGHT, BARRY.
WE DO NEED TO KEEP OUR WITS ABOUT US. WE--

HUP!

OOF!

I'M TELLING YOU, BARRY OLD PAL, IT'S LIKE I'M BEING DRAWN TOWARD SOMETHING. LIKE THE SWORD IS DRAGGING ME TO MY DESTINY!
YOU'RE RIGHT, OF COURSE. IT DOES SOUND CRAZY. BUT IT'S TRUE.

HAVE YOU EVER EXPERIENCED THE CLARION CALL OF FATE, BARRY? OF COURSE YOU HAVE, OBVIOUSLY--
OOF!

HEY! WATCH WHERE YOU'RE GOING, FREAK!

OH, YEAH? WHAT IF WHERE YOU'RE GOING IS WATCHING YOU? THAT'S THE POSITION I FIND MYSELF IN, HONEYBEE.

FRIGGIN' NUTJOB.
OH, YEAH? YOU'RE GOING TO JUDGE ME? YOU'RE GOING TO RATE ME ON A SCALE?
SHOW ME YOUR MATH! WHAT'S THE DENOMINATOR?

NO, BARRY. YOU'RE RIGHT. WE HAVE TO KEEP OUR HEADS DOWN. WE HAVE TO BLEND IN. ACT NATURAL.

MOMMY! IT'S A BIGFOOT WITH A SWORD IN HIS TUMMY!
DON'T LOOK HIM IN THE EYE, SWEETIE. JUST KEEP WALKING.
FRESH APPLES: N. SPY WINESAP ROME MAC
SALE!
ALL PUMPKINS HALF PRICE

DEAR GOD, WHAT IS IT?
DON'T LET IT TOUCH YOU! I THINK IT'S RABID!
I'M WICKED JOHN! I HAVE FEET! JUST WATCH ME!

MY THOUGHT PROCESS HERE, CHUM, IS THAT THE HAND OF DESTINY IS GUIDING ME TOWARD SALVATION.
BY WHICH I MEAN A TOTAL DE-IMPALEMENT OF MY PERSON AND SUBSEQUENT RETURN TO FULL-TIME BADASSERY.

WE DON'T WANT ANY TROUBLE, PAL, BUT I SWEAR TO GOD I'LL BLAST YOU IF YOU TRY ANYTHING FUNNY!

THAT'S A RECURSIVE WITTICISM, ARTEMIS JUNIOR! I ONLY EVER SUCCEED AT ANYTHING FUNNY!
I'D SAY MORE, BUT I DON'T WANT TO OFFEND BARRY'S DELICATE SENSIBILITIES.

HI THERE, FRIEND!
I DON'T KNOW, BARRY. WHAT DO YOU THINK HIS ANGLE IS?

GEE WHIZ, MISTER! ARE YOU OKAY? CAN I DO ANYTHING TO HELP?
GO TO HELL, SCREWBAG!

COME ON, BARRY. WE DON'T HAVE TO TAKE THIS!
OKAY, WELL, IF THERE'S ANYTHING I CAN DO FOR YOU, JUST LET ME KNOW!

HERE YOU GO, MISTER.
I BOUGHT THIS WITH MY ALLOWANCE, BUT YOU LOOKED HUNGRY SO I THOUGHT YOU COULD USE IT MORE THAN I COULD.
FUCK YOU!

WHAT KIND OF TWILIGHT ZONE WACKYVILLE HAVE WE STUMBLED INTO, BARRY?

WHAT IS THIS PLACE?!
Welcome to Canada

SOMEWHERE IN THE WILDS OF A STRANGE WORLD NAMED MAWN-ITO-BAH.
WE MADE GOOD PROGRESS TODAY, DON'T YOU THINK, MacDUFF?
WE COULD HAVE GONE FASTER IF WE'D FLOWN, THOUGH. I STILL THINK IT WAS A MISTAKE NOT TO LET THAT GREEK FELLOW GRAFT WINGS TO YOUR BACK.
WELL, IT'S A MOOT QUESTION NOW. I WON'T HAVE ANY NEED OF WINGS ONCE THIS LAST QUEST IS FINISHED.
SO YOU SAY. I MAINTAIN THAT THEY'D BE MOST DASHING REGARDLESS.
BEFORE WE TURN IN, I THINK IT'D BE A GOOD IDEA TO REVIEW THE LAY OF THE LAND. YOU MENTIONED SOMETHING ABOUT A REFERENCE BOOK?
OF COURSE! AN ALMANACK OF FARAWAY LANDS HORRIFIC AND DEADLY BY A YOUNG UP-AND-COMING WRITER NAMED WULF ALONDAIR LATHE.
IT'S GUARANTEED TO CONTAIN THE MOST PRECISE AND UP-TO-DATE INFORMATION AVAILABLE ON PLACES LIKE THIS ONE.
I ALSO BROUGHT A BUNCH OF THOSE SANDWICH COOKIES YOU LIKE SO MUCH. DOUBLE STUFFED, NO LESS.

HERE'S WHAT YOUNG MASTER LATHE HAS TO SAY ABOUT THE PLACE.
"REPORTS OF THIS DISTANT WORLD ARE SKETCHY AT BEST, BUT THE FRAGMENTARY SOURCES I HAVE UNCOVERED PAINT A VIVID ENOUGH PICTURE IF ONE IS ABLE TO READ BETWEEN THE LINES.
"THE UNKNOWING VISITOR TO THIS LAND DISCOVERS AT FIRST BLUSH AN IDYLLIC PARADISE, FREE OF CRIME, WITH A HEALTHY POPULACE WHOSE KINDNESS AND CLEANLINESS DELIGHT THE SENSES.
"UPON CLOSER INSPECTION, HOWEVER, IT IS REVEALED TO BE A VILE AND CORRUPT BASTION OF HATE, MORE FEARSOME AND DESPICABLE THAN THE NIGHTMARES OF A THOUSAND HELLS.
"THE ILLUSION OF TRANQUILITY AND HAPPINESS IS THE WORK OF THE DREAD RED BRIGADE, THE ARMY OF JACKBOOTED THUGS THAT RUNS ROUGHSHOD OVER THE TERRORIZED POPULACE.
"THE BRIGADE RUTHLESSLY ENFORCES ITS FASCIST SOCIAL PROGRAMS OF POLITENESS AND NEATNESS AS SYMBOLS OF THEIR RIGOROUS ORDER.
"A SINGLE CURT NOD OR MISPLACED NAPKIN MIGHT BE PUNISHED BY SWIFT EXECUTION.
"AND THE LACK OF CRIME IS NO ACCIDENT, EITHER. THOSE APPREHENDED COMMITTING EVEN THE SLIGHTEST PECCADILLO ARE FORCED TO FIGHT TO THE DEATH WITH STICKS ON THE BLEAK SURFACE OF A FROZEN LAKE.
"THE CREED OF THE DREAD RED BRIGADE IS WELL KNOWN AMONG THE FEARFUL INHABITANTS OF THIS BLIGHTED PLACE: WE ALWAYS GET OUR MAN."

COME ON, MacDUFF. HELP ME PUT OUT THIS FIRE. WE DON'T DARE ATTRACT ANY UNWANTED ATTENTION.
IT'S BAD ENOUGH WE'VE GOT TO FIGHT DRAGONS. I DON'T WANT TO TAKE ON ANY OF THESE THUGS TO BOOT.
PERHAPS THAT'S WHAT HAS GOT ME SO UNNERVED, JACK. I'VE HAD THE SHIVERS EVER SINCE WE MATERIALIZED IN THIS WORLD.
I THOUGHT IT WAS THE DRAGON, BUT NOW I'M NOT SO SURE.
COME ALONG, OLD FRIEND. IT'S BEST IF WE KEEP MOVING. I DON'T THINK IT'S WISE FOR US TO SLEEP TONIGHT. NOT IN THIS PLACE.
AGREED.
WE'LL DEAL WITH THE HEINOUS INHABITANTS OF MAWN-ITO-BAH IF WE MUST--
"--BUT IT'S AN EVEN MORE DREADFUL ENEMY WE'VE COME TO FACE, AND IT'S HIM WE SHOULD BE MOST CONCERNED ABOUT."

SOMEWHERE IN MANITOBA...

THIS IS THE THIRD BURNED TOWN WE'VE **BEEN** THROUGH!

WHAT ARE THESE WILY CANADIANS **UP** TO?

BOOK MOBILE

I KNOW WE'RE GETTING CLOSE TO GARY. I CAN FEEL IT. SO, HOW IS IT HE CHOOSES TO LIVE IN SUCH A BARBARIC LAND?
DO YOU THINK IT'S BY CHOICE?

GREAT GRANDDAD'S JUST A NORMAL HUMAN GUY NOW, HILARY. BUT HE COULD BARELY LOOK AFTER HIMSELF WHEN HE WAS THE GREATEST AMONG THE LITERAL POWERS.
HE COULD BE SOMEONE'S HELPLESS PRISONER.

CAPTURED BY THE EVIL NATIVES.
WE SHOULD HAVE CHECKED IN ON HIM YEARS AGO.
DECADES.
WE'RE HIS ONLY FAMILY.

WHAT KIND OF ASSHOLES HAVE WE BEEN NOT TO EVEN MAKE AN ATTEMPT TO SEE HIM ALL THESE YEARS?
AND NOW WE'RE ONLY DOING IT BECAUSE IT LOOKS LIKE HE'S THE ONE WHO'S BEEN HOARDING ALL OF THE TRUE BOOKS WE NEED TO RESTART THE GREAT LIBRARY.

WE ARE NOT GOOD PEOPLE.
BOOK MOBILE

AS HE TAKES WHAT MAY WELL BE HIS FINAL BREATH, MISTER SNIFFLES LOOKS BACK OVER HIS LONG LIFE AND COUNTS HIS REGRETS.
REGRET 1: BEING A SPOKESTISSUE FOR SNIFFLES PLUS WITH ALOE AND LANOLIN.
IT WAS AN INFERIOR PRODUCT-- EVERYONE KNEW IT. AND MISTER SNIFFLES GAVE IT HIS COVETED "MISTER SNIFFLES SEAL OF APPROVAL!"
REGRET 2: SIGNING THAT DEAL WITH THE DEVIL IN WHICH HE RECEIVED FAME AND WEALTH IN EXCHANGE FOR BEING TURNED INTO A GIANT ANTHROPOMORPHIC FACIAL TISSUE.
THAT WAS, HE FREELY ADMITS, A MAMMOTH ERROR IN JUDGMENT.
BUT THAT'S NOT THE BIGGEST ONE, NOT BY A LONG SHOT. THE GREATEST SINGLE REGRET OF MISTER SNIFFLES' LIFE, BY FAR, IS...
REGRET 3: NOT PAYING MORE ATTENTION TO HIS CHILDREN.
MAYBE IF HE'D LOVED HIS KIDS MORE, THEY WOULDN'T HAVE INTRODUCED HIM TO THE DEVIL AND CONVINCED HIM TO GO THROUGH WITH THIS WHOLE TISSUE THING.

LOOK, CAN WE DROP THE GUILT FEST FOR CRAP'S SAKE? WE'VE BEEN WALLOWING IN HOW WE'VE NEGLECTED GARY FOR HOURS.

FINE! THE PAGE SISTERS ARE OFFICIALLY BAD RELATIONS!
STIPULATED AND NOTARIZED!
BUT NOW WE NEED TO FOCUS.

EVERYTHING WE'VE BEEN TRYING TO ACCOMPLISH FOR YEARS--FOR OUR ENTIRE MUNDY EXISTENCE--COMES DOWN TO TODAY.
IF WE CAPTURE THE TRUE BOOKS, WE CAN RESTORE THE GREAT LIBRARY.

WE DO THAT, WITH THE THREE OF US COLLECTIVELY AS THE LIBRARIAN--
A TRIPARTITE GODHEAD.
A TRADITIONAL TRINITY. THE MOST STABLE OF MYTHO-THEOSOMATIC CONSTRUCTS.

--THEN WE BECOME LITERALS AGAIN, AND NO LONGER JUST THREE ANONYMOUS MUNDYS AMONG BILLIONS.

IMMORTALS ONCE MORE.
NO LONGER SUBJECT TO WRINKLES, TURKEY NECKS AND SAGGING TITS.

HONESTLY, HOW DO THE MUNDY'S LIVE LIKE THIS--KNOWING THEY'RE DOOMED TO GET OLD AND UGLY AND BROKEN AT THE BITTER END?
HOW DID WE EVER IMAGINE WE COULD EXIST HAPPILY AS MUNDYS?

WE'LL BE BACK TO LITERAL STATUS IN NO TIME NOW. WE'LL BE YOUNG AND SMOKING HOT AGAIN, ONCE THE LIBRARY IS RESTORED.
ASSUMING WE ACTUALLY RECOVER THE MOTHERLODE OF TRUE BOOKS. ARE WE REALLY GOING TO TAKE THEM FROM GARY AT GUNPOINT?

NOW THAT WE KNOW HE'S THE ONE WHO'S HAD THEM ALL THESE YEARS, SHOULDN'T WE JUST--I DON'T KNOW--WALK UP AND ASK FOR THEM?

REMEMBER, ROBIN, WE DON'T KNOW THAT'S HE'S ACTING ALONE.
THE OPERATIVE THEORY IS HE'S BEEN HELD CAPTIVE ALL THIS TIME BY SOMETHING BIG AND POWER-FUL.

AND EVIL. MAYBE SOME HIGHLY ORGANIZED, WELL-FINANCED UNDERGROUND ORGANIZATION, BENT ON WORLD DOMINATION.
CANADIANS.
EVIL GODDAMN CANADIANS.

READY TO GO?

SOMEWHERE SURPRISINGLY NEARBY...
AT LONG LAST!
AFTER ALL THOSE YEARS STUCK IN THE DINER, WE'RE *FINALLY* ON THE ROAD TO FABLETOWN!

CHEER UP, MISTER WALRUS. WE'RE ON OUR WAY TO THE LONG PROMISED LAND AT LAST.
I'M CHEERFUL ENOUGH, MISTER CARPENTER--EXACTLY AS THE OCCASION MERITS.
KEEP FOLLOWING THE BIRD SPIRIT, MISTER D.
YEAH. NOT THAT I NEED *YOU* TO TELL ME.
AS IF, AFTER FOLLOWING THE BIRD SPIRIT FOR SIX DAYS, ALL THE WAY FROM THE AMERICAN SOUTHWEST INTO THE DARK HEART OF A FOREIGN COUNTRY, TODAY OF *ALL* DAYS IS WHEN I'M SUDDENLY GOING TO *FORGET* THAT--OH YEAH--I'M SUPPOSED TO BE *FOLLOWING* THE MOTHER-PLUCKING *BIRD* SPIRIT.

SO FABLETOWN WAS IN CANADA ALL ALONG.
NO *WONDER* IT'S SO HARD TO FIND.

WHAT ARE YOU GOING TO DO ONCE WE REACH FABLETOWN, PORFIRIO?

OH, THE SAME THING I DID ALL THOSE YEARS STUCK IN THE GOLDEN BOUGHS, FOLLOWED BY ALL THOSE YEARS WE WERE STUCK IN THE DINER, LUDMILLA.

TRY TO STAY **OFF** THE MENU.

I WILL OF COURSE OPEN UP A **HABERDASHERY** TO COMPLEMENT THE GOLDEN SLIPPER SHOE STORE WE'RE TOLD IS THE **TOAST** OF FABLETOWN'S MERCHANT ROW.

ZZZZZZZZZ

MOTHER GOOSE IS **NOBODY'S** FOOL.

I WILL OPEN A DAYCARE SCHOOL.

TO TEACH THE CHILDREN WHO'RE CERTAINLY THERE.

AND TREAT EACH CHILD WITH TENDER CARE.

A BIT FURTHER UP THAT SAME ROAD...
I DARE SAY, IN A LIFETIME OF SHARED RISK, REWARD, SETBACKS AND TRIUMPHS, THIS IS GOING TO BE OUR GREATEST ADVENTURE EVER.

EPIC!
SERIOUSLY THOUGH, I KNOW WE'VE SQUABBLED LIKE HELLIONS OVER THE YEARS, BUT I WANT YOU TO KNOW YOU'RE BOTH THE BEST SISTERS ANY WOMAN COULD EVER HAVE.
I LOVE YOU BOTH--DEARLY. YOU KNOW THAT, RIGHT?

JEEZE-LOUISE, ROBIN!
YOU SOUND LIKE YOU JUST GOT BAD NEWS FROM A DOCTOR. I LOVE YOU TOO, BUT LET'S NOT GET TOO MAUDLIN HERE.

IT'S NOT THE END OF THE WORLD. IT'S THE BEGINNING OF A WHOLE NEW CHAPTER IN OUR LIVES. ONCE AGAIN, THE PAGE SISTERS ARE ABOUT TO KICK ASS AND TAKE NAMES!
WE'RE ABOUT TO BRING LITERALS BACK INTO THIS BLIGHTED PLACE, AND THIS TIME DO IT WITH GRACE, ÉLAN AND STYLE.

RIGHT, THIS CAN'T BE THE END FOR US. IN MANY WAYS, OUR LIFE ONLY BEGINS ONCE WE REESTABLISH THE LIBRARY, WITH SANE PEOPLE RUNNING IT FOR ONCE.
STILL...
...I DO GET THIS ODD, WISTFUL FEELING...

NOT MUCH LONGER NOW, MY DEAR OLD FRIEND. I CAN SMELL IT.
AND IT SMELLS LIKE LIZARD.

DON'T WORRY, BARRY. IF THINGS GET BAD, I'LL PROTECT YOU WITH MY LIFE.

COME ON! WE DON'T HAVE MUCH TIME!
YOU DON'T HAVE TO TELL ME THAT, BIRD. THE QUESTION IS, HOW DO WE BOTH KNOW THAT?

THIS IS A GREAT QUEST WE'VE EMBARKED UPON, JACK. PERHAPS THE GREATEST DEEDS CALL TO US, BECKONING US FORWARD TO HASTEN THE HOUR OF THEIR CONSUMMATION.

ANYONE WANT THE RADIO ON?

CHRIST ALMIGHTY, THIS ROAD IS BUMPY! YOU *SURE* WE'RE HEADED IN THE RIGHT DIRECTION?
STAY THE COURSE, MISTER D. NOT MUCH LONGER NOW.

WE'RE NOT GOING TO FABLETOWN, *ARE* WE?
NO, MY GOOD MAN. I'VE BEEN TELLING YOU THAT ALL ALONG.
WE WERE NEVER *MEANT* TO FIND IT.

I DO **NOT** LIKE THIS WORLD ONE **BIT**. IT SMELLS OF SNOW AND SMOKE AND ILL TIDINGS.
AS YOU SAY, MISS.

DON'T YOU WORRY, LITTLE NIBLET. EVERYTHING'S GOING TO BE JUST **FINE**.
JUST FINE.

THE STAGE IS SET. THE PLAYERS ARE TAKING THEIR PLACES. THE CURTAIN IS ABOUT TO RISE.
I'VE THOUGHT ALL ALONG THAT *I* WAS THE ONE PULLING THE STRINGS, BUT THIS IS **FAR** BIGGER THAN ANYTHING I COULD EVER HAVE MANAGED.
WHO'S PULLING MY STRINGS? BECAUSE THIS IS GOING TO BE **EPIC!**

COME ON, JACK! WE'VE GOT TO GO! WE NEED TO BE FAR AWAY BEFORE OUR ADVERSARIES ARRIVE.
IF WE PUT OUR MINDS TO IT, WE CAN BE IN ANOTHER WORLD BY TOMORROW!

NO, OLD FRIEND. IT'S TOO LATE FOR THAT NOW.
I'VE SPENT YEARS AMASSING THIS GREAT HOARD AND I COULDN'T LEAVE IT NOW EVEN IF I WANTED TO, WHICH I DON'T.

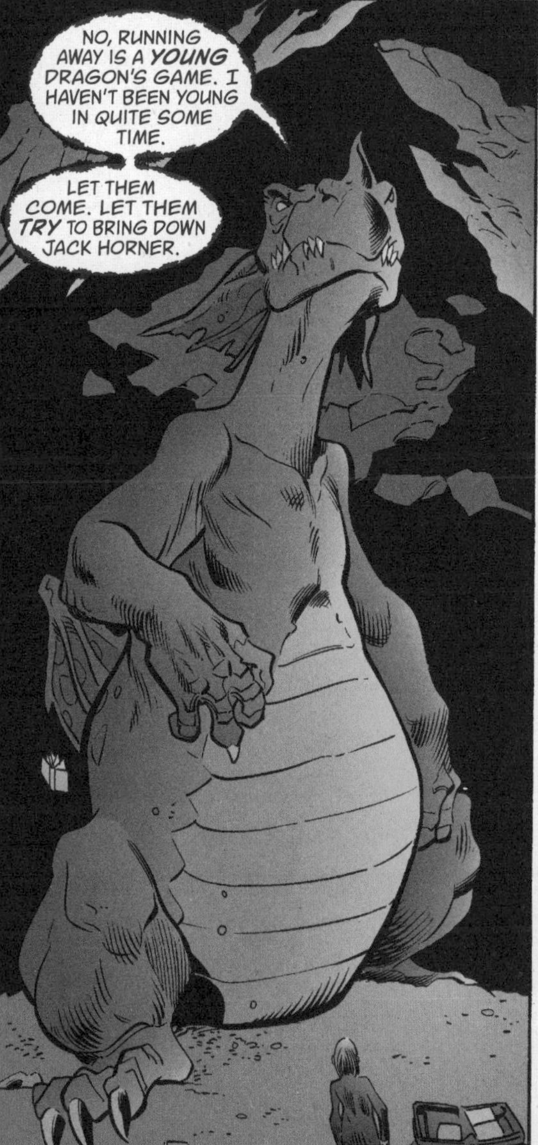
NO, RUNNING AWAY IS A YOUNG DRAGON'S GAME. I HAVEN'T BEEN YOUNG IN QUITE SOME TIME.
LET THEM COME. LET THEM TRY TO BRING DOWN JACK HORNER.

THEY'LL FIND I GIVE AS GOOD AS I GET.
BRING 'EM ON.

WELL, WHAT DO YOU KNOW?

A MINIATURIZED BLUE OX

THE FOURTH ESSENTIAL COMPONENT
IN THE MOST EPICALLY NIFTY JACK OF FABLE
STORY IN THE HISTORY OF THE UNIVERSE!

NEXT: The Shakespearean Ending

"AT LAST!
AT LONG LAST!
IT'S TIME TO
COLLECT!"

SO...
...IT ENDS HERE.
THE DRAGON, HIS SIDEKICK, A NEMESIS, & THEIR COWS
THE FINAL INDISPENSABLE COMPONENTS IN THE LAST JACK OF FABLES STORY OF ALL TIME!

GREETINGS, OH GREAT AND DIRE WYRM OF DEATH AND DESTRUCTION. I AM A KNIGHT ERRANT, DISPATCHED TO WRITE AN END TO YOUR FOUL DEPREDATIONS.
IF YOU'VE GODS, I'LL ALLOW YOU A MOMENT TO PRAY BEFORE WE BEGIN. THERE'S NO REASON WE CAN'T BE CIVILIZED ABOUT THIS MORTAL AFFAIR.
SINCE YOU DESERVE TO KNOW SOMETHING ABOUT YOUR ADVERSARY OF THE DAY, I AM THE LIBERATOR OF ATHEBORE, THE SLAYER OF THE HOLO-CAUST BEAST OF JANNE SECUNDUS.
I BROUGHT DOWN THE TOPLESS BLACK TOWER OF GOTHAL NEGROS, AND SCOURED THE DRIFT WORLDS OF THE PLAGUE SCYRAT LEAGUE.
OOH, AND TELL THEM ABOUT THE SARUKAN ADVENTURE! I REALLY SAVED OUR BACON IN THAT ONE!
BOOM MOBILE
DO I KNOW YOU? YOU LOOK FAMILIAR.
THIS IS FABLETOWN? I THOUGHT IT'D BE MORE OF A... YOU KNOW, TOWN.

I HAVE A BAD FEELING ABOUT THIS, JACK. VERY BAD.
DON'T WAIT. DON'T TALK. TAKE THEM OUT. BURN THEM ALL DOWN.
"A FIERCE DRAGON. A MIGHTY VETERAN KNIGHT, THE HERO OF COUNTLESS ADVENTURES. TWO TITANS MEET UPON THE FIELD OF BATTLE. THE GREAT CONTEST COMMENCES.
"WHO WILL STAND? WHO WILL FALL? WHO WILL ARISE VICTORIOUS WHEN THE SMOKE FINALLY CLEARS?"

"A TRIO OF WOMEN WARRIORS ENTERS THE FRAY, EQUIPPED FOR BATTLE. BUT FOR WHICH SIDE? ARE THEY OUR FAIR KNIGHT'S AMAZONIAN SQUIRES, OR MISTRESSES OF THE GREAT REPTILE'S MESMERIC THRALL?"
HOLY CRAP ON A STICK! GARY HAS A DRAGON GUARDING THE BOOKS! HAS THIS NEBBISH THING BEEN AN ACT ALL THIS TIME? IS HE ACTUALLY SOME KIND OF DIABOLICAL MASTERMIND?
I DON'T CARE WHAT HE IS. HE'S STANDING BETWEEN US AND THOSE BOOKS, AND IF HE AND HIS DRAGON DON'T MAKE WAY, THEY'LL GET A HAIL OF LEAD FOR THEIR TROUBLE.
I HAVEN'T COME THIS FAR AND SACRIFICED THIS MUCH TO BE PUT OFF BY ONE MEASLY DRAGON.
SO, SHOULD WE TRY TO TALK TO HIM FIRST, OR SHOULD WE JUST LET 'EM HAVE IT?

AND WE'VE GOT OUR ANSWER! HE VIXENESQUE VIRAGOS HAVE ICKED THINGS OFF WITH A TRULY MPRESSIVE DISPLAY OF GUNFIRE!"
YOU DON'T SIT DOWN FOR A NICE CHAT WITH A DRAGON. YOU SLAY THE SON OF A BITCH!
RRRROARRR!
JACK! GET DOWN!
SIGH
SO MUCH FOR PARLEY.
GERONIMO!
HEY! IS THAT OUR NEPHEW? IS THAT JACK FROST?

ENOUGH SCREWING AROUND. LET'S GET TO THE KILLING!
THAT'S IT, JACK! KILL THEM! KILL THEM ALL!
GET YOUR FILTHY FANGS OFF HIM, YOU DASTARD!
"AND WE'RE OFF! THE DRAGON LOOKS DARN IMPRESSIVE TAKING THE FIRST SNAP OF THE GAME. HE'S IN GREAT FORM!"

OH, BOY! THINGS HAVE TAKEN A NASTY TURN EARLY ON! THIS IS CLEARLY SHAPING UP TO BE A FIRST-CLASS GRUDGE MATCH!"
RRRRRRROOOOWWWRRR!
THEY'RE DISTRACTED!
WE HAVE OUR OPENING!
GO FOR THE BOOKS!
AAAAGGHH!
JACK! I CAN'T GET A CLEAR SHOT!
COVERING FIRE! ROBIN?
ALREADY ON IT!
EAT HIM! EAT THE BOY!
"OH, WILL YOU LOOK AT THAT! THE PAGE SISTERS HAVE EXECUTED A SURPRISE END-AROUND RUN!"

"HOLD ON! IS THAT A LEGAL MOVE? IS THAT ALLOWED?"
"YOU'RE DAMN RIGHT IT'S ALLOWED! THIS IS *PRO* BALL, WULF. YOU WANT A NICE CLEAN GAME, YOU GO PUT ON A *DRESS!*"
YOU HOMICIDAL DICK-WEASELS!
YOU'R *BOT* DEAD
AAAAGGGGHHH!
YOWZA!
THAT OUGHT TO TEACH YOU SOME MANNERS!
I THINK I CAN FEEL IT. CAN YOU FEEL IT?
YEAH. SOMETHING LIKE--?
VICTORY.

ND NOW A DARK HORSE AM RUSHES ONTO THE ELD! LOOKS LIKE WE'VE OT OURSELVES A BALL GAME, FOLKS!"
MOVE OUT! MOVE OUT!
THAT DRAGON IS THE ONLY ONE WHO NOWS THE SECRET WAY O FABLETOWN! IF HE DIES, THEN OUR DREAM DIES WITH HIM!
SO I SAY TO YOU NOW--IN THE NAME OF ALL YOUR HOPES ND DREAMS, IN THE NAME OF OUR FUTURE, IN THE NAME OF FABLETOWN ITSELF--SAVE THAT DRAGON!
I DO BELIEVE I'LL STAY RIGHT HERE. I'M A LOVER, NOT A FIGHTER, DEAR!
THIS IS MADNESS. MADNESS AND TOMFOOLERY! I NEVER SHOULD HAVE CLIMBED ABOARD THIS DAMNABLE BUS!
NICE! I COULDN'T HAVE SAID IT BETTER MYSELF, RAVEN.
WHAT A BUNCH OF RUBES!
YOU FOLKS GOT ANY SORT OF A CLUE 'BOUT WHAT MIGHT BE GOIN' ON HERE?
ACTUALLY, WE WERE HOPING YOU COULD TELL US. WHAT MANNER OF ALTERCATION IS THIS?

OH, THAT'S GOTTA HURT!
IF YOU'RE JUST JOINING US, I'M WULF ALANDAIR LATHE DOING THE PLAY-BY-PLAY OF THE BIG GAME--AND BOY OH BOY HAVE WE GOT A REAL BARN BURNER GOING ON UP IN MANITOBA!
JOINING ME HERE IN THE STUDIO, WE'VE GOT JACK HORNER PROVIDING COLOR COMMENTARY, AND BABE THE BLUE OX WITH THE PLAYER STATS AND SIDELINE REPORTS.

NOW, JACK, THIS ONE STARTED UGLY AND HAS JUST GOTTEN UGLIER. WALK US THROUGH THIS AND TELL US HOW THINGS ARE SHAPING UP SO FAR.

WHAT IS THIS BULLSHIT?
FIRST THEY MAKE ME FAT. THEN THEY TURN ME INTO A DRAGON. AND NOW THAT THEY FINALLY BRING BACK THE NARRATIVE CAPTIONS, THEY DON'T EVEN LET ME DO THEM!
AND TO ADD INSULT TO INJURY, WHEN I FINALLY DO GET A WORD IN EDGEWISE, I DON'T EVEN GET TO DO PLAY-BY-PLAY. I'M STUCK DOING COLOR COMMENTARY ON MY OWN DAMN SHOW!

AND THAT'S WHEN BRUNHILDA SAID, "THAT'S NOT RICE, THOSE ARE MAGGOTS!"

AT LONG LAST! AFTER ALL THESE YEARS!
AFTER A HUNDRED DISAPPOINTMENTS AND FALSE LEADS!
THE TRUE BOOKS! THOUSANDS OF THEM! ENOUGH TO RESTART THE GREAT LIBRARY!
CAN YOU FEEL IT? I FEEL YOUNGER ALREADY! I THINK WE'RE IMMORTAL AGAIN. I FEEL LIKE A LITERAL AGAIN!

THIS IS WHAT IT WAS ALL ABOUT?
YOU SHOT ME FULL OF HOLES IN ORDER TO STEAL MY BOOKS?
NOT MY GOLD. NOT MY TREASURE HOARD. BUT A BUNCH OF USELESS, WORTHLESS BOOKS?
I'M SICK AND TIRED OF THESE DAMNED BOOKS! I SHOULD HAVE DONE THIS DECADES AGO!
OH NO!
NO!
NOT NOW! NO AFTER AL WE'VE--!

LOOK! THE DRAGON'S BACK
OUT OF THE CAVE AND BOY
DOES HE LOOK MAD!"
"WOULDN'T YOU BE, WULF?"
WALRUS!
I'VE ALWAYS LOVED YOU!
TAKE CARE OF THE OYSTERS!
FABLETOWN-AUTHORIZED GODS AND DEMONS, SAVE US!
MOMMY!
I THOUGHT HE WAS ON OUR SIDE!
HANG ON, JACKIE BOY. LET ME CAUTERIZE YOUR WOUND.
I KNOW IT HURTS LIKE THE DICKENS, BUT--
SSSSSSSSSSSS
I CAN--TAKE THE PAIN, MacDUFF. JUST GET IT--UNH--DONE!
THEN FIND WHERE THE FULMINATE BLADE LANDED.

"AND HERE'S THE TIN MAN--A SURPRISE DRAFT CHOICE FROM AN OBSCURE CLUB, WHOSE GLORY DAYS ARE LONG BEHIND THEM."
"YOU'RE RIGHT THERE, WULF. IT'S MY UNDERSTANDING THAT THEY HAD TO TAKE HIM IN ORDER TO GET THE LION."
YOU SHOULD HAVE TAKEN MY SWORD ARM, DRAGON. IT'LL BE THE LAST MISTAKE YOU EVER MAKE.
THAT SON OF A BITCH RAVEN LIED TO US. THAT DRAGON'S NO SAVIOR--HE'S WALKING, FLAMING DEATH, AND IT'S OUR DUTY TO TAKE HIM DOWN.
IF WE'RE TO DIE, THEN LET'S DIE LIKE LIONS!
JUST A SECOND, FIERCELY. I'VE GOT AN ATTACHMENT I'VE NEVER USED. I'M NOT EXACTLY SURE WHAT IT DOES, BUT IF EVER THERE WAS A TIME TO FIND OUT, IT'S NOW!
WATCH THE FEET! WATCH THE FEET! INNOCENT BYSTANDER DOWN HERE!
DO NOT PRESS
SPLA
GARY! YOU UP THERE?
IT'S ME--YOUR COW CONNECTION.
I KNOW IT'S BEEN A WHILE, BUT I JUST CAME INTO A SHIPMENT OF QUALITY MEAT ON THE HOOF AND SINCE YOU WERE ALWAYS ONE OF MY BEST CUSTOMERS, I THOUGHT I'D GIVE YOU FIRST DIBS!
INTERESTED?

HEY! COWS!
BAD ATTACHMENT! BAD ATTACHMENT! OH, THE BOVINITY!

"OH MY, WILL YOU LOOK AT THIS! THE PAGE SISTERS COME ROARING BACK INTO THE ACTION!
"WE THOUGHT THEY WERE EMOTIONALLY INJURED, OUT FOR THE DURATION, BUT THEY'RE FIGHTERS. THEY KNOW THE GAME ISN'T OVER 'TIL THE LAST WHISTLE BLOWS!"
"FUNNY YOU SHOULD SAY THAT, WULF. ALL THREE OF THEM HAVE BLOWN MY WHISTLE. IF YOU CATCH MY DRIFT."
SCREW IT!
WITH THE TRUE BOOKS GONE, WE'RE MUNDYS FOREVER NOW, DOOMED TO DIE!
SO EVERY-ONE'S DOOMED TO DIE WITH US!
OH, THE INDIGNITY!
THE HUMANITY!
NOT... MY...LUCKY... DAY...!
GREAT BIRD SPIRIT! WHY?
WHY DID YOU LEAD US INTO THIS DEATH TRAP?
NO PARTICULAR REASON. I THOUGHT IT'D BE FUNNY.

KAY, THAT WAS CLEARLY AN ILLEGAL
! I CAN'T BELIEVE HE DIDN'T GET
ENALIZED ON THAT PLAY! JACK, WHAT
AN YOU TELL US ABOUT HUMPTY DUMPTY--
OWN TO ALL HIS FANS AS 'MISTER D'?"
"HE'S A DIRTY PLAYER, WULF. ALWAYS HAS BEEN."
I WASTED THE BEST YEARS OF MY LIFE IN THAT HELLHOLE YOU CALLED A "RETIREMENT VILLAGE!"
YOU WANT TO GO OUT IN A BLAZE OF GLORY? I GOT YOUR BLAZE RIGHT HERE, BITCHES!
AND I GOT A POCKET FULL OF SUPERGLUE, SO I AIN'T FEARING NOTHING!
THOOM!
RISCILLA!
NOOOOOO!
WHY DO YOU LOOK SO DAMN FAMILIAR? YOU'RE A HANDSOME YOUNG BUCK, I'LL GIVE YOU THAT.

"NOW, THIS IS A FAIRLY COMPLEX PLAY WE'RE LOOKING AT HERE. WALK US THROUGH IT, JACK, AND TELL US WHAT WE'RE SEEING."
"HELL IF I KNOW, WULF. MY ATTENTION SLIPS CONSIDERABLE WHEN THE DRAGON ISN'T ON."
ULK!
AHA! TWO DOWN, ONE TO GO!
SUPER-GLUE THIS, YOU BASTARD! YOU SHOULD HAV BEEN TIGER FOO DECADES AGO!
DAMMIT! I DIDN'T WANT TO BE FRIED! I DIDN'T WANT TO BE SCRAMBLED! I ALWAYS THOUGHT I'D BE OVER EASY!

MAZING! MID-PLAY, THE NE-ARMED KID CALLS AN DIBLE! **GOD,** HOW I LOVE THIS GAME!"
MacDUFF, HOLD OFF THE DRAGON FOR A MOMENT!
FAMILY VENGEANCE TAKES **FIRST** PRIORITY!
FIERCELY LION! WHEN NEXT WE MEET, IT SHALL BE IN **OZ!**

"THE OWL MacDUFF IS A FASCINATING STORY, JACK. HE IMPRESSED ABSOLUTELY NO ONE IN HIS ROOKIE YEAR, BUT IN HIS LAST FEW OUTINGS HE'S REALLY PROVED HIMSELF TO BE A PREMIUM ASSET TO THE TEAM. YOUR THOUGHTS?"
"SURE. WHATEVER. SAY, DO WE GET COCKTAIL SERVICE UP HERE IN THE BOOTH?"
I'M ON IT, BUDDY!
WICKED JOHN IS HERE!
NOW IT CAN BEGIN!
OW!

TONIGHT I FEAST ON FLAME-BROILED OWL!
I LOVE YOU, JACK FROST! BE STRONG! LIVE WELLGGLLglrRp!
MacDUFF!
BARRY! PULL HARDER! I SWEAR TO CHICKENS YOU'RE THE RIGHTFUL KING OF ENGLAND!
WICKED JOHN? COULD IT POSSIBLY BE YOU?

"WE'VE CLEARLY GOT A HISTORY-MAKING GAME ON OUR HANDS, FOLKS. WE'RE GOING TO SIT BACK FOR A MOMENT AND WATCH ALONG WITH YOU AT HOME AS THIS EPIC CONTEST UNFOLDS."
YOU'LL DIE FOR THAT! I SWEAR IT!
WAIT A MINUTE. JACK FROST? JACK FROST?!
JACK! LOOK OUT! HE'S COMING RIGHT AT YOU!
SORRY, WICKED JOHN. I HAVE TO BORROW YOUR SWORD FOR A MINUTE! I'LL GIVE IT RIGHT BACK! HONEST INJUN!
WHUMPF

SCHWWAAANG!
NO ONE HARMS MY JACK AS LONG AS *I* DRAW BREATH!
OKAY, *THAT* DIDN'T TURN OUT GOOD.

KRA-KOOM!

FIRST MacDUFF AND NOW THE FULMINATE BLADE?!
DIE, YOU MONSTER!
VRRAAC
GARY?

LITTLE BUDDY!
FWOOOOSH
GROWWWR!

YOU THINK FIRE CAN HARM ME?
I'M JACK FROST! I'M THE ONLY HEIR TO THE HOUSE OF WINTER, COLD AND ICE! I'M THE LIVING EMBODIMENT OF ANTI-HEAT!
NOT EVEN DRAGON'S FIRE WILL CAUSE ME ANYTHING BUT A MOMENT'S DISTRACTION!

ENOUGH!
LET'S END THIS!

SUITS ME.

"OH! OH MY! I HAVE TO TELL YOU, I'M SPEECH-LESS. I CAN'T THINK OF ANYTHING TO ADD TO THIS TERRIBLE MOMENT.
"THEY TELL ME WE WANT TO GO DOWN TO BABE ON THE SIDELINES FOR SOME POST-GAME REACTION. WHAT DO YOU HAVE TO TELL US, BABE?"

EVEN AS HE REACHES THE END OF HIS LONG PROFESSIONAL CAREER, ALONSO THE CRUELTY-FREE PIRATE HAS NEVER STOPPED LOOKING FOR KINDER, GENTLER FORMS OF PIRACY.
EVEN USING THE MOST HUMANE METHODS, ALL THAT GRAPPLING AND SWORD-FIGHTING AND ENFORCED PLANK-WALKING CAN STILL CAUSE UNWANTED INJURY, BOTH PHYSICAL AND PSYCHOLOGICAL!
THUS, ALONSO HAS DECIDED TO GIVE INTERNET PIRACY A WHIRL. IT'S LESS VIOLENT, TO BE SURE.
AND YOU DON'T EVEN HAVE TO GO OUT TO SEA TO DO IT, WHICH IS GOOD FOR ALONSO BECAUSE THE SALT AIR MAKES HIS BAD KNEE FLARE UP.
SO YOU CAN IMAGINE ALONSO'S HORROR WHEN HE LEARNED THAT INTERNET PIRACY IS IN MANY WAYS EVEN MORE CRUEL THAN THE TRADITIONAL KIND.
YOU CAN ONLY CUT OUT A MAN'S HEART ONCE, YOU SEE, BUT YOU CAN CUT INTO HIS PROFITS FOREVER!
AND THAT'S HOW ALONSO FINALLY WENT BROKE--MAILING GUILT-INSPIRED ENVELOPES OF CASH TO KENNY G.
WHAT CAN ALONSO SAY? HE CAN'T GET ENOUGH OF THAT SMOOTH JAZZ!

"OH, MY. I DIDN'T THINK--THEY'RE ALL DEAD. UHM--I DON'T KNOW WHAT TO SAY. ANY COMMENT, JACK?"
"THOSE SICK BASTARDS WENT FOR THE SHAKESPEAREAN ENDING.
"NO ONE GOT MY PERMISSION FOR THAT."

"IS THERE ANYONE WHO ESCAPED FROM THE GOLDEN BOUGHS WHO SURVIVED TO TELL THE TALE? ANYONE AT ALL?"
FREE AT LAST!
FREE AT LAST!
01

I'VE EFFECTED MY DARING ESCAPE FROM THE GOLDEN BOUGHS!
IT'S BEEN A LONG HAUL. BUT I STUCK TO THE PLAN. I NEVER WAVERED. AND NOW, FINALLY, ALL THAT PATIENCE AND HARD WORK HAS PAID--
01

SPLAT!

LEPUS
MOVERS

HOLD ON! WHO'S THIS COMING ONTO HE FIELD IN THE FINAL MOMENTS OF HE FOURTH QUARTER? THEY LOOK LIKE-- VELL, CALLING A SPADE A SPADE, THEY OOK LIKE A BUNCH OF DEVILS! JACK? CARE TO ENLIGHTEN US?"
"UH--YEAH, WELL, THE THING IS...
"SEE, WAY BACK WHEN, I GOT MYSELF INTO A FIX OR TWO AND, IN ORDER TO GET OUT OF IT I--"
AT LAST! AT LONG LAST!
IT'S TIME TO COLLECT!

"EXCUSE ME FOR A MOMENT, FOLKS. I NEED TO GO TAKE A *LEAK*."
HOLD ON THERE, MISTER SCRATCH! *I* HAVE CLAIM TO HIS SOUL!
AS DO I.
ME, TOO!

I THINK WE SHOULD CUT THE CARDS TO SEE WHO GETS THE BOY'S SOUL.
NO WAY, NICK SLICK! YOU'RE A NOTORIOUS CARD CHEAT!
WE'RE ALL *THE DEVIL.* OF COURSE WE CHEAT!
TRUE. THERE *IS* THAT.
I THINK TO BE FAIR, THE MOST MASSIVE AND *TERRIFYING* OF US SHOULD PREVAIL.
LOOK AT ME! I GOT THE HORNS, THE HAIRY CHEST, THE MUSCLES, AND THE BEST MINIONS! MY BOTTOM HALF IS MADE OF *FIRE!* I WIN!
♪

IN THE NEXT THRILLING ISSUE, I BECOME A HIGH POTENTATE OF MARS, BANG A BUNCH OF GREEN MARTIAN HOTTIES, GET INTO SCUBA IN A BIG WAY, JOIN THE MARINES, WIN A PIE-EATING CONTEST, CLIMB MOUNT EVEREST BLINDFOLDED, REANIMATE GARY'S CORPSE AND TURN HIM INTO A LIVING MUPPET, ENSLAVE THE ENTIRE HUMAN RACE, AND LEARN FRENCH.
WHAT? YOU THINK JUST BECAUSE THE SERIES IS OVER I'M GOING TO STOP DOING STUFF?
YOU ARE NOW LEAVING
JACK OF FABLES
We hope you've enjoyed your stay!

THE END

YOU'LL NEVER FORGET THE FIRST

AMERICAN VAMPIRE
VOL. 1

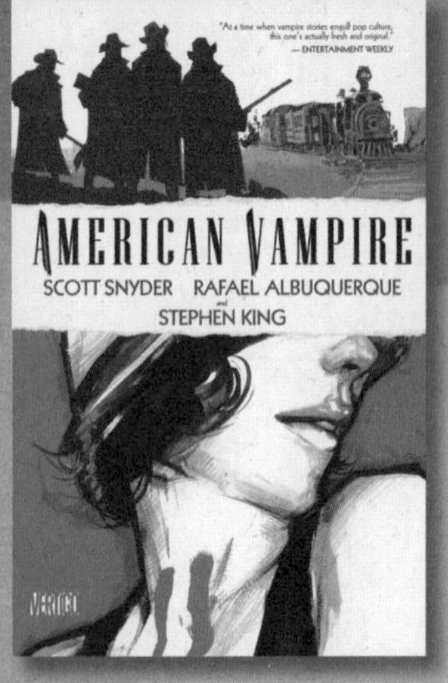

DEMO
VOL. 1

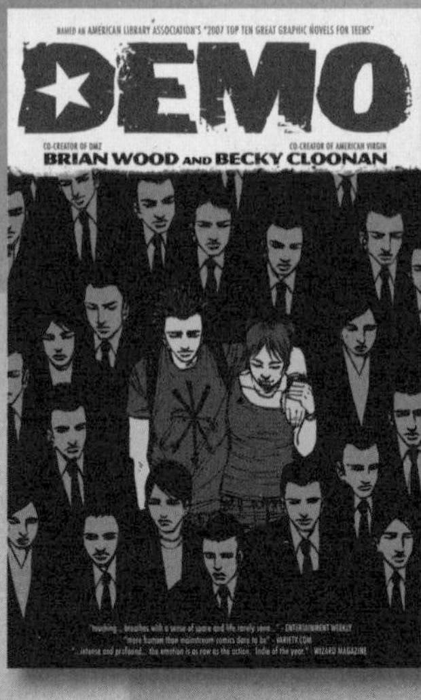

THE LOSERS
BOOK ONE

THE UNWRITTEN VOL. 1:
TOMMY TAYLOR AND
THE BOGUS IDENTITY

SWEET TOOTH VOL. 1:
OUT OF THE DEEP WOODS

UNKNOWN SOLDIER VOL. 1:
HAUNTED HOUSE

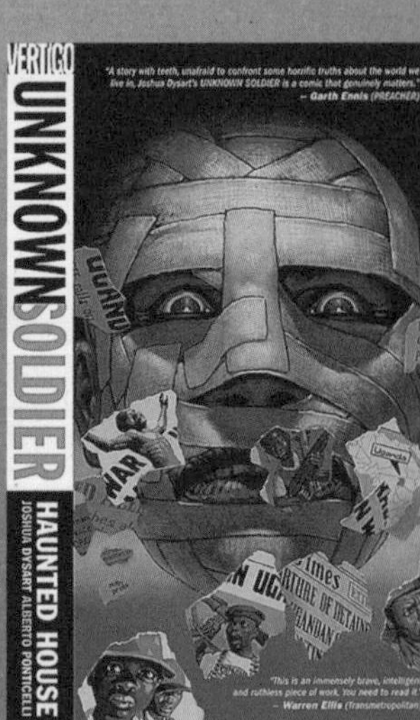

GO TO
VERTIGOBOOKS.COM
FOR FREE SAMPLES OF THE FIRST ISSUES OF OUR GRAPHIC NOVELS

Suggested for Mature Readers